VIN VIGNETTES

Stories of Famous French Wines

Sarah Jane English

To my cousins Nancy and Dan with fondest best wishes

Sarah Jane

EAKIN PRESS
Austin, Texas

FIRST EDITION

Published in the United States of America
By Eakin Press, P.O. Box 23066, Austin, Texas 78735

ISBN 0-89015-452-X

To Myra and Clarence English
in gratitude for my heritage
and my opportunities

CONTENTS

Acknowledgments   vii

Introduction   ix

Burgundy   1

Bordeaux   31

Champagne   53

Rhône   65

Loire   75

Historic Names   85

Index   87

v

About the Author

Sarah Jane English has had a long-time fascination with the famous wines of France, and as a non-professional wine connoisseur, has a wide-based knowledge of the wine industry.

The author takes part in wine tastings nationwide, is a lecturer and consultant on writing and is in demand for her programs on wine. A busy magazine writer, Sarah Jane has delved into the budding Texas wine industry while writing on a variety of subjects, including interviews with famous personalities.

In the past year she has sold some thirty magazine articles, including seven cover stories. She has completed three novels and a number of short stories, one of which was published in 1984.

A graduate of The University of Texas, she served as editor of the *Alcalde*, the alumni magazine, for three years before becoming a free lance writer.

A native of Dallas, the author is a member of an historic Texas family which includes Daniel Boone of Kentucky fame and James English, probably the first circuit-riding Methodist minister in Texas. Her father was a pioneer in the bus and trucking industry in Texas and one of the first Texans to pilot his private plane for business purposes.

A resident of Austin for the past sixteen years, she is a member of the Junior League of Austin, Delta Delta Delta alumnae, Daughters of the Republic of Texas, Daughters of the American Revolution, Heritage Society, and Les Amis du Vin. She was also a graduate of Highland Park High School in Dallas.

—Photo by Gray Hawn

Acknowledgments

Any book, I believe, is the product of multiple joint efforts. Some of my help came in the form of encouragement from friends, and the reaffirmation of my ability by colleagues and respected authorities who gave me their guidance. Too, valuable resource persons gave their time and knowledge for the improvement of this book. I have been blessed with a plethora of such personages. It would take a book the size of *Vin Vignettes* to list all the names contributing to my good fortune, and it grieves me not to have the space. My love to all those not mentioned, and you well know who you are.

In addition, I give heartfelt thanks to those of paramount significance: Charles W. Ferguson, Maggie Cousins, Liz Carpenter, Denise Schmandt-Besserat, Hélène and René Philipponnat, the Champagne firms of Moët & Chandon and Pol Roger and De Meric, Chantal and Claude Colas, Jean-Marie Guillas of Mâcon, F. Protheau et Fils, Les Caves Delorme-Meulien, Henri N. Thomas-Moillard and Louis Latour. Also, Leon Adams, Ed Auler, Rose Baxter, David Francis, Barbara Wilson Fuller, Coleen and Dick Hardin, Ralph Hutchinson, Remi Krug, Lloyd Mardis, Stanley Marcus, Ruth Wilson Melton, Margrit and Robert Mondavi, Marvin Overton, Simone Poulain, Mary Renfro, Jean Robitscher, Mollie Hawkins Sharpe, Peter Sichel, and June and Bryan Spires.

Foreword

If it is true that champagne was the wine of kings and if we can call it the "exquisite ambassador of French perfection," then could not we say of Sarah Jane English that she is the "exquisite ambassador" of French wines.

Without getting lost in boring technical details, Madame English knows how to discuss the originality and distinctive quality of great French wines as well as the reasons for their prestige throughout the world. We can't thank her enough for this.

I was particularly impressed that her first visit to Champagne was to meet with the descendant of one of the oldest families of Champagne (the Philipponnat family first settled in Aÿ in the 16th century).

I was also impressed to find out that this contact was the result of a friendship between Sarah and Denise Schmandt-Besserat. Originally from Champagne, she has lived in the United States for several years where she participates in scientific studies.

Much has been said about the *Civilisation du Vin*. And it's true that there are numerous shared traits among the inhabitants of European wine regions. My deepest wish is that this book, because of the bonds it will strengthen between Old France and the New World, have the greatest success and that it will contribute both to the development of a Franco-American friendship and to the development of this *Civilisation du Vin*, of which we, native of Champagne, are especially proud.

RENÉ PHILIPPONNAT
Former *chef de cave* of Moët & Chandon

Champillon, France
July 12, 1984

Foreword

If you are looking for that one brief introduction to French wines — one that will take much of the confusion out of the plethora and complexity of French names — *Vin Vignettes* is the answer to your quest.

Sarah Jane English has drawn upon her background in the French language, her frequent sojourn in France and her love and enthusiasm for French wines to provide a geographic guide to the wine regions of France, accompanied by a little history and some of the lore surrounding some of the famous names. The pronunciation guide is invaluable, a sure route to avoiding the embarrassment of provoking a shudder from a wine steward (who may speak only wine label French) by a fumbled or mispronounced name.

If it is true that Americans will not order wines the names of which they cannot pronounce, *Vin Vignettes,* is sure to increase the sale of French wines.

The suggestions for combinations of wines and food are also helpful guides to choosing wines to accompany food, or, as some of us are fond of doing, choosing foods to go with wines we have already chosen.

Another attractive feature of the book is its brevity, which makes it easy to use and assures that it will be consulted frequently. If the novice masters *Vin Vignettes,* thereby ceasing to be a novice, he or she can move on to more detailed study with a firm foundation on which to build.

RALPH B. HUTCHINSON, PH.D.
California State
Polytechnic University

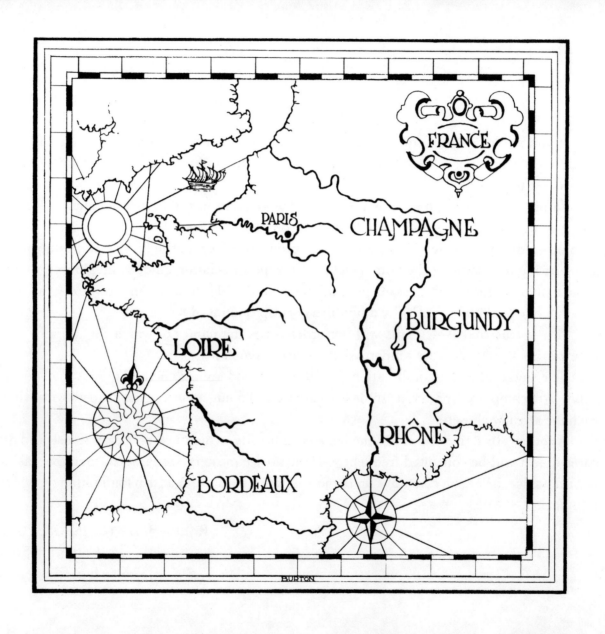

Introduction

My affinity for France and things French began when I was a child growing up in Dallas, Texas. From the first grade onward at Miss Hockaday's School for young ladies, Mademoiselle Moulin taught us the French language, French culture and the delightfully French *le bonheur* — a delicately balanced form of personal happiness reserved for mature Frenchmen. She exuded it, and her indoctrination overwhelmed me completely. The inimitable Mademoiselle was enthusiastic, effusive, and infectious, and my classmates and I were imbued with an uncanny sense and appreciation of things French.

Additionally, I took ballet lessons — taught in French — from Helen and Gladys Kingsbury. If we performed well and curtsied nicely *après la lecon,* we received a delicious bon bon. The dish of tasty morsels was placed strategically, dangling the reward before our eyes with every pirouette and encouraging excellence. I've been a frustrated ballerina ever since.

I guess Neiman-Marcus reinforced my Frenchification with its marvelous French fortnight — a two-week extravaganza during which the downtown store displayed every conceivable quality French item for the delight of the customers. Neiman-Marcus and Hockaday girls were synonymous.

When I first traveled abroad as a young adult, I automatically headed for France. It was in the intimate bistros and elegant restaurants of Paris that I was introduced to the product of the grape — France's noble wines. I have been studying and learning about them ever since, because it is truly a pleasant lifetime endeavor.

Since that initial holiday, I've returned to France every year or so for twenty years. Several trips were specifically to see vineyards, explore wineries and taste the regional wines. The most recent winery/vineyards visit (May-June 1983) included specific research for *Vin Vignettes*.

Friends requested that I write this book. Part of the reason they gave for wanting it was the mystique that surrounds wine. There's such ceremony and so many unknowns, especially since drinking wine on a regular basis is a fairly new phenomenon for Americans. Frenchmen refined the practice and the idea, but they unintentionally confused the pleasure with their difficult language. For many Americans, French wines are unpronounceable. Yet because French vineyards produce some of the world's most famous wines, my friends were curious about them and wanted to be able to recognize and pronounce the names on wine lists. I thought (and hope) that this book would be an interesting and fun way to solve the problem.

It is brief and limited in scope because of a second request from friends. They were totally overwhelmed by the lengthy, detailed and technical tomes which exist. Many complained about "overkill" — much more information than they wanted to know. Others were bored with the presentation of material. Some simply couldn't find what they wanted; and so, the request for this book.

I also hope *Vin Vignettes* will make wine a conversational subject. Many people enjoy drinking wine, but they feel uncomfortable talking about it. The reason is that such talk usually involves judgment of the wine's characteristics — descriptions of colors, bouquet and aroma, and the various tastes. Many people lack the experience and vocabulary to feel at ease describing wine, but anyone can learn a story about a vineyard or a wine and feel perfectly comfortable telling it. As a matter of fact, that person is usually considered the life of the party.

In addition to the guide for pronouncing the wine names and towns that are included in each section, I have given general characteristics and food suggestions in the tables which end the sections. In the event that someone wants to enjoy the wine Napoleon favored one night, or that preferred by Charlemagne or some other historic notable on another evening, there is a list of such personages and their wine preferences. Friends gathering around my table insist they adore learning about wine in this manner — associating them with historic people and events. It certainly makes for a lively and interesting *petit souper* at my home, and I hope that the same proves true for the dinner parties *chez vous*.

 A votre santé!

VIN VIGNETTES

Stories of Famous French Wines

FRANCE

PARIS CHAMPAGNE

BURGUNDY

LOIRE

RHÔNE

BORDEAUX

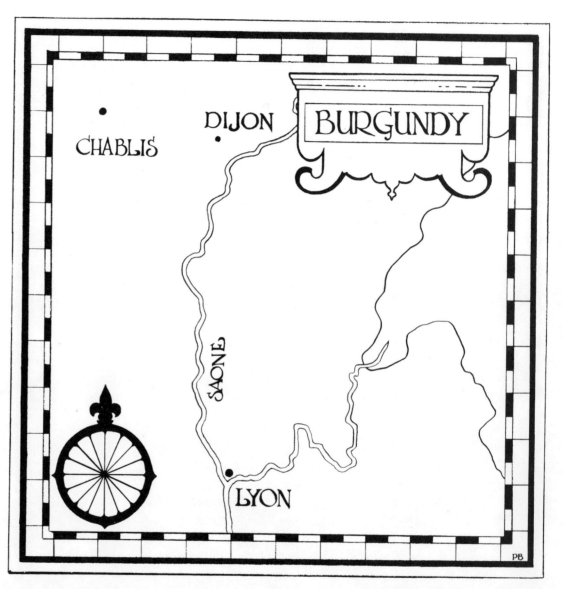

CHABLIS DIJON BURGUNDY

SAONE

LYON

PB

Burgundy

The ancient province of Bourgogne has been chopped up and sub-divided time and again throughout the centuries. The Celts, Romans, the Germanic tribes of the Burgundii, and the Franks, all took turns with the landscape. After 1790, post Revolutionary bureaucrats partitioned Burgundy along with the rest of France into 90 administrative *départements*. Now the present regime of Mitterrand et al., is reorganizing things again. The one reliable designation of French land seems to be the wine districts. In Burgundy, there are five distinct ones: Chablis, Côte d'Or [the "Golden Slope" being divided into two sections: Côte de Nuits (the grand reds) and the Côte de Beaune (the great whites)], Côte Chalonnais, and the Mâconnais and Beaujolais. There are other, smaller administrative units within the *départements* called communes, that is, a town or village and its surrounding lands. To add to the confusion, communes often take their names from the dominant town which may have attached to it the name of the most prominent vineyard in the area. Thus, Gevrey became Gevrey-Chambertin; Vosne became Vosne-Romanée; Puligny became Puligny-Montrachet. In the case of Chablis, it is the name of the wine, the village, the commune and the district.

There are many vineyards within each commune. Unlike Bordeaux, however, where each major vineyard is owned by the person responsible for producing its wine, Burgundian vineyards have multiple owners. And while Burgundy produces only burgundy, just as Bor-

1

deaux produces only bordeaux, these myriad small landholders — because of their individual methods of viticulture and wine production as well as the location of their particular plot — make extremely different wines.

The small farmers do not produce enough wine for them to bottle themselves, but rather they sell to *négociants,* who blend, bottle, and sell to the public. Most have integrity and make a good wine. But in this way, also, some inferior types and grades get blended and sold as burgundy. This wine, however, has no resemblance to genuine burgundy, the best of which is incomparable, while the less distinguished bottles can be very poor indeed. Burgundians say: *Respectez les crus.* The remark advises one to know specific *climats* (vinyards). Another bit of important advice is to know a reliable *négociant* (shipper). There are a number of them who produce wine from the 1200 Burgundian appellations: Joseph Drouhin, Louis Latour, Louis Jadot, Moillard, and Bouchard Père et Fils. In addition to identifying the vineyard, labels on outstanding bottles name the commune and use terms that help identify quality: *Appellation Contrôlée, mise au domaine or mis en bouteilles par* (a name) or *le propriétaire.*

Although Burgundy does not have a classification like that of Bordeaux, the wines do have four levels of quality: regional wines, village wines, first growth wines (*Premiers Crus*) and great growths (*Grands Crus*). Burgundy produces approximately two percent of France's wine and about half that amount is Beaujolais.

Mention the word Burgundy and most people see red — red wine, that is. Actually, a more correct mental image would envision land — narrow islands of vineyards in the eastern section of central France. This ancient area produces some of the world's finest red wines, but especially white wines, a preference oenophiles (wine lovers) have argued for centuries.

Oenophiles aside for the moment, disputes of other sorts have plagued Burgundy. Even its name comes from one of the feuding, barbarous Germanic tribes (Burgundii) that invaded Gaul after the dissolution of the Roman Empire. After the onslaught by the Roman legions, the Burgundii had found the Celts reasonably tamed. They had staggered under the relentless blows of Julius Caesar, and the youthful Gallic chieftain, Vercingetorix, had finally lost to the general in 52 B.C. Of course there were several hundred years between the visits of the Romans and Burgundii. Those years helped the Gallic-Roman evolve, he became a somewhat more subdued wine-drinking warrior than in earlier days. And so, the Burgundii were not the first fighters or wine enthusiasts on French soil. Just as the Celts, the Romans qualified.

To Romans, however, neither topic nor pursuit was safe from controversy. For example, before his death while watching Vesuvius erupt, the ancient scholar Pliny had compiled an encyclopedia of natural science. In it he disagreed with his learned predecessor Livy, about who first introduced the vine to Gaul. But whoever the original bearer, there's no doubt that the conquering Romans spread the magic of the grape, and vines were planted throughout the Empire. Wine, just as gold and textiles and spices, represented ancient world wealth.

The Romans established the vine and, perhaps in tribute, the Burgundians remembered. A commune and several renowned vineyards have been appropriately christened to preserve the Roman effort. Within the commune Vosne-Romanée are three outstanding vineyards. La Romanée, remarkable for its size (two acres) as well as its wine, is one; but Romanée-Conti is considered by most great wine connoisseurs to be the best red wine of France. It is certainly one of the most scarce and expensive. The *climat* (Burgundian term for vineyard) measures 328 by 590 feet and yields approximately 7,500 bottles. Alexis Lichine, author and wine expert, calls it "the most precious vineyard in the world." Apparently Madame de Pompadour thought so. She wanted to buy it. But her master, King Louis XV, let his cousin — Louis François de Bourbon, Prince de Conti — win the day. The Prince, after all, was of royal blood, a distinguished general and statesman and, incidentally, directed matters of secret diplomacy for the King.

In the 13th century, Romanée-Conti and the surrounding vineyards were the property

4

of the Priory of Saint Vivant — hence the name of the other Romanée *climat,* Romanée Saint-Vivant. The wines were greatly admired by the dukes of Burgundy, so much so that they ordered decrees to protect the grape (Pinot Noir) from an encroaching variety (Gamay) that yielded more juice but less quality. Alas, the old tribal instincts overcame the monks and they decided to liquidate their valuable *climats* in order to equip themselves for a Holy Land pilgrimage. The new owner, the man who subsequently sold the vineyard to the Prince of Conti in 1760, planted the vines that had the unique experience of surviving the deadly phylloxera — plant lice that attacked virtually all French vineyards in the 19th century. Romanée-Conti, however, was a victim of the Revolution — it was nationalized — but eventually it became private property again and today belongs in part to a descendant of that post Revolutionary purchase.

Wine authorities agree that some Vosne-Romanée wines are the ultimate representatives of great Burgundian bottles and among the best reds in the world.

After the Huns drove the less violent Burgundii southwest into Gaul, they merged with the Romanized Celts. The two peoples seemed to have common traits — a bellicose verve and a love to till. The Gallo-Romans invited the evicted agriculturists to stay and help cultivate their fields — for a share of the profits, naturally. And so, the Kingdom of Burgundy evolved and the territory of the dukes preserved the viticultural traditions established in Roman times. As a matter of fact, Nuits-Saint-Georges, where wine was made during the Roman period, continued to flourish so well that Louis XIV's royal physician, a man named Fagon, prescribed its wine for the King because of its "dry, tonic and generous qualities." The full-bodied reds are as admirable today.

The Franks were another Germanic tribe that looked southwestward. Following their fifteen-year-old leader Clovis I, they founded the Frankish Empire and extended it over the next several centuries by conquest. The first dynasty, the Merovingians, divided the realm into a number of kingdoms and their constant fighting, et cetera, made their civilization barbaric. It was the Church that preserved a semblance of Gallo-Roman culture, for Clovis had married a Christian and Clothilde converted him from paganism. In the 8th century the Carolingian dynasty gained control and helped the Frankish Empire achieve its zenith of power. And it was the son of Pepin the Short — a boy named Charles, later called Charlemagne — that accomplished that feat. According to his chronicler, Eginhard, the King of the Franks was "six feet four inches tall and built to scale. He had blond hair, animated eyes, a powerful nose and presence always stately and dignified. He was temperate in eating and drinking and kept in good health despite every exposure and hardship. He took vigorous exercise, and behind his poise and majesty were passion and energy." (Will Durant, *The Age of Faith*; p. 470; Simon and Schuster; N.Y. 1950).

A white wine from a vineyard Charlemagne once owned bears his name, Corton-Charlemagne (Côte de Beaune); and, just as the traits he embodied, the wine is high quality, distinctive, well-balanced, has great breed and is more steely than soft. In keeping with his tireless effort to spread and support Christianity, Charlemagne deeded his vineyard to the Church via the Abbey at Saulieu. The idea seemed to catch on and before long the Church was rich in vineyards, notwithstanding Charlemagne's demise or the Dark centuries that followed.

The monasteries became the handmaiden of the vine. A group of Benedictines, monks unusually adept at vine-growing and wine-making, lived in Cluny, a village in the heart of Burgundy whose church was the largest in the world. Bigger did not necessarily mean better, especially during the Dark Ages when every institution reached its nadir. All elements were attracted to Cluny, a cultural center and crossroad of the world, and the practices of the multitudes as well as the clergy offended some of the monks. It was one thing to drink a little wine and quite another to get drunk and like it. Anyway, these dissenting monks moved several miles east into a marshy area and called themselves Cistercians. Reluctant at first to plant vines after seeing the evils of wine, they eventually were persuaded (12th C.) because nothing else would grow successfully. These Cistercians planted the Clos de Vougeot and their agricultural skills turned a wasteland into a viticultural wonder. With 125 acres, it is the largest of the Burgundian vineyards and continues to exact the same admirable respect it has always garnered. Just as in previous decades, passing troops of French soldiers still honor the noble vines with a reverential salute.

Clos de Vougeot has one of the few châteaux in Burgundy. It turned out to be an architectural monstrosity, an evidence in stone against the sin of pride. According to Burgundian legend, after additional acres had been bequeathed to the brotherhood in the 16th century, the monks decided the property ought to have a press house and château. The abbot assigned an artistic brother the job of drafting plans. He labored and labored and loved his labor, fervently affixing his name to the finished product. Such immodesty, indeed audacity, won him only wrath from the hierarchy, and as justified punishment, the abbot gave the blueprints to a committee, no doubt assuming what havoc such a move would create. Well, it did. As only a committee can botch, the plans loomed with protean faults and the structures were built with each one of them intact. Poor soul, upon seeing the revision the original architect died instantly from mortification.

The Château de Vougeot is a clubhouse of sorts for the *Chevaliers du Tastevin*. This society of vine-growers, winemakers, and oenophiles holds seated banquets for 500 and frequent wine tastings to keep the world aware of Burgundian wines. And, they purchased the château for the purpose. The official garb of the brotherhood is showcase quality: silver tastevin (tasting cup) dangling from a golden striped, lobster red ribbon against a black apron, their voices raised in song, and their eyes bright beneath their billed, black berets. It is a fitting toast to a vineyard that has produced quality wine for eight centuries. No longer the domain of the church, Clos de Vougeot has an estimated 66 owners now, and understandably, bottles vary. Still, the wine is famous, and deservedly so: a full-bodied burgundy with a distinct, floral perfume.

With less colorful celebrants, but certainly with equal if not greater import, are two vineyards in the commune of Gevrey-Chambertin. Again, land was a gift to the Church, this time from Almagaire (the Duke of Burgundy in 630) to found the Abbey of Bèze. The monks took to tilling with an unprecedented devotion, especially after they discovered what extraordinary grapes/wine the land would yield. The abbot ordered a wall *(clos)* to be built around it, and hence, Clos de Bèze. But the wall didn't keep the eyes and nose of the peasant Bertin from acknowledging the great vineyard from his pasture next door. The story goes that the peasant also planted Pinot Noir, and five years later Bertin's field *(champ de Bertin)* produced grapes that made equally divine wine. Chambertin is called *un grand seigneur,* which means it is a great lord of Burgundy. Some say, additionally, the appellation derives from the fact that it was Napoleon's favorite red wine, an attachment that enhanced Chambertin's reputation.

The two vineyards, Le Chambertin and Chambertin-Clos de Bèze, have 70 acres between them and yield approximately 7,600 cases in a good year. Many consider Chambertin the greatest red wine in Burgundy. One vine-grower is reported to have said after drinking it: "One seems to have swallowed the good Lord himself wearing velvet pants."

The unforgettable Chambertin — a full and beautifully balanced deep red wine with perfectly blended characteristics — nonetheless has competition, for Burgundy is replete with good wines and extraordinary circumstances.

In Chambolle, for a strange example, there's a confusion of vineyards and châteaux. Actually, there are only two of each involved, but in both instances they share the same name. Not that sharing names is totally unusual for vineyards. (Beaune and Corton both have Bressandes and Clos du Roi. That's why it is important to know the commune and the vineyard.)

Anyway, concerning the buildings, the older Château de Chambolle-Musigny has been owned by the Mugnier family for over a century, but with unfortunate lapses in their occupancy. Massive and functionally rectangular, the Germans confiscated the nineteenth century structure for barracks during World War II. When they vacated it, the French and Americans took turns using it. All this tramping in and out didn't help the antiquity, but somehow the place held up in spite of it. In 1950, however, a softer treading came back to the estate and mercifully permitted it to do what it does best — use the vat rooms and magnificent cellars for the glory of wine. One viniferous product is from the alluring vineyard Les Amoureuses, "women in love," a name as soft, charming and feminine as the delicate wine. Another wine under the watchful care of Domaine Mugnier and other vineyard owners is called simply Les Musigny. It is noted among the usually sturdy red burgundies for its extraordinary elegance and finesse, one of Burgundy's most memorable. And what about Chambolle-Musigny's other château that is called by the same name, Château de Chambolle-Musigny? It is a modern building which the Mugnier family wishes the owner would call something else. Since copyrights don't exist for châteaux names, they must live with the confusion.

In the case of the vineyards, Bonnes-Mares and Les Bonnes-Mares, it is the proximity as well as the names that further confuse, for their acreage is split between two communes — Bonnes-Mares (about 33 acres) in Chambolle-Musigny and Les Bonnes-Mares (4½ acres) in Morey-Saint-Denis beside the ancient Clos de Tart. The twin vineyards are members of that select group of Burgundian wines (31 out of 100s) so famous they need only the vineyard name on the label, not the commune.

As for the Clos de Tart, it is named for the female counterpart of the Cistercian order (Bernardines de l'Abbaye de Notre-Dame de Tart) and, consequently, its wines are sometimes referred to as the "ladies' wines." The term is misleading. These nuns made big, robust wine but with an extreme and special subtlety. Perhaps their most characteristic contribution to Clos de Tart is its exceedingly delicate ability to grow old graciously.

While both sections of the Côte d'Or produce red and white wines, the northern portion (Côte de Nuits) is most renowned for reds just as the southern part (Côte de Beaune) is celebrated for its dry whites. Nonetheless, it was a red wine that early on brought attention to the Côte de Beaune. The place was Pommard; the time was the 17th century. Just as the many French protestants of that time, the villagers of Pommard were suffering religious persecution. Louis XIV had revoked the Edict of Nantes in 1685 (issued almost 100 years earlier by Henri IV to recognize two religions in France). And so, the Huguenots — representing all classes — made their exodus from France. They took their treasured Pommard with them into Belgium, the Netherlands, Switzerland, Britain and America, sharing it and making it famous among their newfound friends. Pommard's reputation has stood the test of time well and today it is one of the most widely demanded beverages of old Bourgogne. Such ubiquity of familiarity and fame, however, can prompt fraud, so labels should be checked for the distinguishing comments mentioned earlier that will identify genuine Burgundian products.

For the most part, oenophiles agree that the Côte de Beaune is homeland for the greatest dry white wines in the world. The Chardonnay grape which produces them has a natural proclivity for ancient Burgundian soil. This urge together with a balanced topographic climate of high altitude and muted sun help create the perfect wine.

The Côte de Beaune is named for the undisputed capital of Burgundian wine, Beaune. Over the years it has been a hotbed for wars and intrigues, especially when the noble dukes of Burgundy were overcome by their ambitions. In their quests to rule, walls and castles went up and down with an undulating regularity. Additionally, pestilence added to the misfortunes, plaguing the medievalist for 32 years of the 14th century and 41 years of the 15th century. Rampant disease, no doubt, contributed to the construction of the Hospices de Beaune, a charity hospital built in 1443 that still functions today.

The hospital is funded in part by revenues earned from its vineyards — gifts of land donated by generous Burgundians throughout the Côte d'Or. Wines made from vines close to Beaune are sold as Beaune (or the vineyard name may appear after Beaune); but, the Hospices vinifies its own wines and sells them under the name of the land donor — Nicolas Rollin, Docteur Peste, Charlotte Dumay, and so forth — not the vineyard. In this way, Hospices wines come from Meursault, Pommard, Corton and other communes in the district. The price of these wines, more symbolic than noteworthy, determines the value of all Côte d'Or wines and the event for it is the annual wine auction at the Hospices during November. It is a gala to match any gala and the *Trois Glorieuses* (lavish banquets, parades, tastings, dances, et cetera) lasts for three glorious days. The first banquet takes place at the Clos de Vougeot in an elaborate hall the day before the auction opens. The second banquet is held in the Hospices cellars at the conclusion of the auction. The next day Meursault hosts the third banquet and has dubbed it *La Paulée*. It refers to a custom that town's vineyard workers still observe; that is, a rest (*paula* is Greek for "rest") in the middle of the day. The habit is sanctioned because of all Burgundian *climats,* the steep, sloping hills of Meursault are the most difficult to tend. But, surely the two names that bring ecstatic palpitations to every wine lover's palate are Meursault and Montrachet. Both names, theoretically, are of Latin origin.

Meursault, strangely enough, derived from *muris saltus,* or, the leap of the mouse. It seems the Romans constructed two types of roads when they moved into Gaul. One was for the horsepowered vehicles of the day — wagons and chariots and such. The natural flat landscapes were best suited for these super highways, open plains or ravines or wide places. The Roman foot soldier, however, wanted the shortest distance between two points in case a hasty retreat seemed the better part of valor. This sort of path cut across a Burgundian stream, narrow enough for the legions to leap it. And so the place was dubbed *muris saltus,* only a short mouse's leap from one side to the other. In spite of the Roman attempt to latinize their tongues, the Celts held on to their language. They preserved their way of saying things and their unique character: a cavalier attitude towards law and organization; a boastful, argumentative, rowdy approach to life, and an independent mind that set about molding Latin into French. *Muris saltus* became Meursault.

The important thing about Meursault, however, is the wine. The Cistercians brought their special viticultural acumen to the area during the 12th century and Meursault has been benefitting from the Benedictine defectors ever since. The production is large (second only to Pommard in the Côte de Beaune) and 97% of it is white (while Pommard is red). The labels on the best bottles name the vineyard and the commune and must come from a reliable *négociant*.

Just a *muris saltus* away from Meursault is Montrachet. Opinions differ as to how its name came to be. One holds that the word comes from the way Burgundians of the Middle Ages said *mons rachicensis*, Latin for "Bald Hill," the state of Montrachet's slopes. The Romanized Celts pronounced it *montrachet* (both *t*'s silent). Another school of thought believes the Latin derivative was *mons racemus, racemus* meaning grapes and eventually wine. In any event, the wine is young by most Burgundian standards since it dates from the 17th century. There's a saucy story connected with the vineyards of the world's greatest dry white wines. It seems a wealthy landowner decided to share his prosperous hillsides with his brood of offspring. In dividing the estate, he quite wisely selected the best vineyard for himself, Montrachet. To his oldest son, a distinguished *chevalier,* he gave the next best estate, Chevalier-Montrachet. But there was another son, sadly of questionable birth — the rather embarrassing by-product of a wayward escapade. To him the father gave the lusty vineyard appropriately called Bâtard-Montrachet. The remaining several daughters, all unmarried, received the last portion of land and it was named Les Pucelles for their virginal statuses. Significantly, each vineyard reflects the character of its appellation. Montrachet is the most distinguished with its regal flavor and impressive, lingering aftertaste. Chevalier-Montrachet has great class and finesse. The Bâtard-Montrachet is a bit dryer, more vigorous with a seductive bouquet. And the delicate Les Pucelles in Puligny-Montrachet has a lovely trace of softness, a beguiling freshness.

There are other renowned vineyards in the side by side communes of Puligny and Chassagne. Les Demoiselles once lay beside Chevalier-Montrachet, but the numerous ribald comments were so offensive the name was changed to Le Cailleret (from the verb to curdle). Les Chalumeaux (a reed) and Les Folatières (playful) also command respect. Nevertheless, Montrachet reigns supreme. It is rated by the authorities as one of the most magnificent vineyards in all of Burgundy. Apparently the French government agreed with the designation. In 1962 it spent over $1,200,000.00 to divert a major highway system around the rare acreage. The author of *Les Trois Mousquetaires* and *Le Comte de Monte Cristo*, Alexander Dumas, allegedly said: "Drink Montrachet only on one's knees with the head bared."

Of the five Burgundian wine districts, the Côte d'Or is by far the most illustrious. The

16

noble reds of its Côte de Nuits and the regal whites of its Côte de Beaune have been categorized among the classics.

Nonetheless, some of the wines of the four remaining districts may sound more familiar and be more popular as well as available. Certainly Chablis and Beaujolais have a ring of familiarity for American wine drinkers. And just as with the completing regions in old Bourgogne — Côte Chalonnais and Mâconnais — they share a history of Celts, Romans, Burgundii and monks.

One monk from the Cistercian order, Saint Bernard, founded the Abbaye de Fontenay not far from Chablis. He practiced a form of "if you can't take the country out of the boy, take the boy out of the country." His reputation for proselytizing was legion, and upon hearing of his proposed visit, mothers, wives and young women lived in fear of losing their men to the abbey. Indeed, when he began his career at Cîteaux, St. Bernard brought friends and relatives with him, including several of his brothers. Eventually he convinced his immediate family they were in peril of the eternal fires of hell unless his mother and sister retired to a nunnery and his father joined a monastery. They did. Like many righteous persons — if not fanatical, at least excessively devout — the monk was relentless in his acquisitions. Monastic orders were a heaven of a sort amid the wars and chaos that prevailed. In addition, the puny, austerely ascetic St. Bernard eschewed the secular world with an energetic piety that captured converts. The order grew. After prayer, fasting and solitude, a monk's work in the fields represented his only form of self-expression; and so, the vineyards thrived.

One might think that Saint Bernard had endowed the region's Chardonnay with a portion of himself. Chablis has a taste characterized as *pierre à fusil*, or flinty, and austere with a touch of astringency. The comparison ends there. The wine is delicate, clean and fresh, while the monks seldom bathed. One hesitant recruit even complained that he couldn't endure the vermin in his ecclesiastical habit.

In the United States almost any white wine is called chablis. The difference, however, between such wine and the genuine article must be experienced. The color of French chablis is a pale straw tinged with slight green. It is unusually dry (with wine, dry is the opposite of sweet but does not mean sour), and has a fleeting perfumed bouquet. Some say the commune of Chablis is shaped like a shell, a factor that somehow helped determine it would be the perfect drink to accompany oysters, clams, lobsters and such. Whatever the reason, it does. The name of any of these vineyards on a bottle of chablis insures blissful sipping: Blanchots, Les Clos, Valmur, Grenouilles, Vaudésir, Les Preuses and Bougros.

While the northernmost Burgundian district of Chablis is famous for its crisp white wines, Beaujolais, the southernmost Burgundian district, celebrates its abundant light reds. Many of these wines are swallowed (not sipped) when only months old and they are seldom

18

kept for over two years. Beaujolais produces young, fresh, fruity wines, the *vin bourru* (carafe wine) of Paris cafés and a favorite that compliments most any dish.

During the 10th century, Beaujolais was established as a buffer zone between two larger, bellicose provinces. Basically, it was protected from the chaotic conditions around it — invading Northmen and Arabs, the Church/state struggles, Charlemagne's incompetent and quarrelsome successors — because of its less important position. Consequently, the people of Beaujolais developed the traits that have characterized them and their wine for centuries, and a tale symbolizing the qualities is passed down to their children.

One day a 14th-century ruler of Beaujolais was seated comfortably at court reviewing the times. Apart from having to succumb to the fairly new invention of spectacles, things were well. The silk industry and trade fairs at nearby Lyon were extremely successful; King Philip IV had built an indoor tennis court in Paris (the harbinger of modern racket games and lawn tennis); the Black Death had killed a third of England's population (a fate that helped France in the Hundred Years' War); lute playing was popular; the first francs had been coined; the Bastille was under construction, and the French Court had scheduled its first gala ball. Suddenly, a breathless messenger dashed before the ruler.

"Sieur! Mercenaries are sacking Anse!"

"Outrageous! Bring my armor and my horse! Sound the trumpets and drums to call my serfs!"

And so, the entourage marched off *en masse* to save the Beaujolais town. Upon seeing the noble approach, the soldiers barricaded the town walls and got ready for warfare.

"Surround these walls, men!" the *Sieur* commanded. "We'll destroy this town and everything in it!"

"But *Sieur*. It's one of *your* towns," a peasant suggested.

"Hummm. Good point, Jacques."

After a moment, he called for a parley. Being more good- than bad-humored, the lord didn't really want to fight. In addition, he didn't want to destroy one of his towns just to get rid of the rabble, especially at considerable cost to himself.

A plunderer peaked over the wall to answer his summons. "Yeah? What do you want?"

"My treasurer has just been figuring the cost of this battle. In lieu of fighting, I'm prepared to offer you a reasonable sum to leave in peace and never return."

"Just a minute,' he replied.

"Mumble, mumble, mumble."

"All right. We accept."

With the *bonhomie* and easy way typical of these charming people, the entourage rode off.

The wine, too, is called pleasant, agreeable, refreshing, and light without a trace of harshness. They say the wines of Saint-Amour (sacred love) are gentle and soft and caressing; most amiable to drink. Fleurie (flowery) has a fragrant bouquet while Moulin-à-Vent (from a windmill that overlooks vines) is full and vigorous. The Romans were here too. Juliénas derives from Julius Caesar, and it is said that the wine's youthful fruitiness survives to a lusty age. Other memorable Beaujolais wines are Morgan, Chénas, Chiroubles, Brouilly, and Cóte de Brouilly. These are the *Grands Crus* of Beaujolais followed in importance by Beaujolais-Villages and Beaujolais.

Different grapes need different climates and soils. In Beaujolais the usual Burgundian limestone departs and the soil shifts to granite. The Gamay adores it and thrives. However, north of Beaujolais is limestone country and the addictive Pinot Noir and Chardonnay dominate the fields.

In Mâconnais, it is the Chardonnay that merits so much attention and some trace the reason to the Solutréan epoch. During that Stone Age period, a prehistoric group lived in Solutré, hence the name. Remains of their culture indicate that they enjoyed magic, believed in the supernatural, lived in man-made shelters, sewed skins with their own invention (bone needles), much to the misery of womankind, and ate wild horse meat. Perhaps the buried bones from this last indulgence enhance the white wines of Mâconnais with additional calcium soil. This is the land of the famous *Pouilly-Fuissé* (poo-yee fwee-say) and, at least in

America, the less well-known *Pouilly-Loché* and *Pouilly-Vinzelles*. The genuine *Pouilly-Fuissé* must come from one of the following communes: Pouilly, Solutré, Chaintré, or Vergisson.

To the north of Mâconnais is the Côte Chalonnais. Just as the other two southernmost Burgundian districts, if offers larger vineyards with less fame and that combination adds up to fewer dollars for very pleasant, agreeable wines. Four communes produce Chalonnais. Rully (mostly sparkling), Givry (predominantly red), Montagny (exclusively white), and Mercurey (the best known, 95% red).

In their day, the Romans constructed a temple to Mercury, messenger of the gods and lover of many goddesses. He invented the lyre, was the first to make fire and also was the patron of commerce. The temple has been replaced by Dionysus's favorite work of art, vineyards. Dionysus was the youngest of the twelve Olympians; the god of wine and ecstasy. He endowed Midas with the proverbial golden touch, but doubtlessly kept enough for his own judicious use in his agricultural work. The wine drinkers of Chalonnais and indeed of all Burgundy and the world as well, will be eternally grateful.

22

great red wine Pinot Noir **BURGUNDY** Côte d'Or (Côte de Nuits section)

Township (commune)	Vineyard (climat)	General characteristics	Food suggestions
Gevrey Chambertin chev-ray shahm-baire-tan	Le Chambertin Chambertin-Clos de bèze Chambertin cloh-duh-bez	great bouquet, full, balanced, unified characteristics	beef roasts and steaks, pâtés, Brie, Epoisses, Reblochon, Double Gloucester, Roquefort
Morey Saint Denis more-ray san day-nee	Bonnes Mares bawn-mar Clos de la Roche cloh duh la rahsh Clos Saint Denis cloh san day-nee Clos de Tart cloh duh tar	subtle, firm, delicate yet robust, class, stamina	lamb, veal, fowl Camembert
Chambolle Musigny sham-bowl moose-een-ye	Les Musigny lay moose-een-ye Les Amoureuses lay za-moo-roose Les Bonnes Mares lay bawn mar	distinct bouquet, delicate, elegant, finesse, least masculine of all red burgundies	quiche, mutton, mushrooms, veal, stews, Emmenthal, Gruyère, Saint Paulin
Vougeot voo-show	Clos de Vougeot cloh duh voo-show	perfumed bouquet, full, balanced	game, cassoulet, spicey beef, rib eye

Township (commune)	Vineyard (climat)	General characteristics	Food suggestions
Vosne Romanée vone row-may-nay	Romanée Conti row-mah-nay- con-tee La Romanée La Tâche la tashh Les Richebourg lay reesh-borgg La Romanée Saint Vivant la row-mah-nay san vee-vawhn	soft, finesse, delicate, beautifully balanced	vension, duck, beef steaks and roast, Brie, Roquefort
Nuits-Saint-Georges newee san shoresh	Le Saint-Georges luh san shoreshs Les Cailles lay kie-yuh Les Pruliers lay prewl-yea Les Porrets lay poh-ray	firm, full-bodied, pungent bouquet, slow-maturing	beef, game, stews, Citeaux, Emmenthal, Appenzeller, Stilton

white, Chardonnay red, Pinot Noir **BURGUNDY** Côte d'Or (Côte de Beaune section)

Township	Vineyard	General characteristics	Food suggestions
Aloxe-Corton ahl-loss kor tawn	Les Bressandes (red) lay bree-sand Le Corton (red) luh kor-tawn Le Clos du Roi (red) luh cloh dew rah Corton-Charlemagne (white) kor-tawn sharl-mahn	noble, full, well-balanced, great breed, long-lived	pheasant, guinea hen, rib roast, turkey, smoked meats, Roquefort, Brie
Pommard (reds) poh-mar	Les Epenots lay zeh-pay-no Le Clos Blanc luh cloh blanh Les Rugiens-Bas lay roo-gem bah	good bouquet, fairly deep color, full, pleasant aftertaste	mutton, braised beef, fowl, pâtes, Emmenthal
Volnay (reds) vawl-nay	Les Champans lay shawn-pan Les Caillerets lay kie-yea-ray	fine bouquet, rounded, balanced, quick maturing	rack of lamb, turkey, roast beef, Coulommiers, Gruyère

25

Township (commune)	Vineyard (climat)	General characteristics	Food suggestions
Meursault (white) mair-so	Clos des Perrières cloh day per-ry-aire and Les Perrières Les Charmes lay sharm	delicate bouquet, dry, well-balanced, full-bodied	shellfish, *escargots,* sweetbreads, chicken livers, ham, Port-Salut
Puligny-Montrachet (white) poo-lean-ye mawn-rash-shay and Chassagne-Montrachet shass-ahnya mawn-rash-shay	Chevalier-Montrachet she-val-yea Les Chalumeaux lay sha-loo-moh Bâtard-Montrachet bah-tarr Folatières foh-la-te-air Montrachet mawn-rash-shay Bâtard-Montrachet Montrachet Criots-Bâtard-Montrachet cree-o bah-tar mawn-rash-shay	great bouquet, dry, pale golden color, tremendous class and flavor, touch of softness	lobster, special fish dishes, bisques, smoked salmon, pork, Appenzeller, chicken, Cantal, Reblochon, Chèvre

BURGUNDY Côte Chalonnais

Mercurey (red) mer-kyuh-ray	Clos-du-Roi cloh dew rah Clos des Fourneaux cloh day fore-no	considerable perfume, light, short-lived	cold meats, duck, turkey, goose, pork, Edam, Coulommiers, Munster
Givry (red) she-vree	Clos-Saint-Pierre cloh san pea-aire Clos-Saint-Paul cloh san puhl	firm, robust, needs aging	spicy beef, game
Montagny (white) mawn-tan-ye	Sous-les-Roches sue lay rahsh	light, fresh, crisp	ham
Rully roo-yee	vauvry voh-vree	dry, fruity, also sparkling	fish dish

BURGUNDY Mâconnais

Pouilly poo-yee	Pouilly-Fuissé poo-yee fwee-say	fine bouquet, light, rounded, dry, pleasant	fish, cream soups, crab, barbecue chicken, Port-Salut
Solutré sew-lou-tray	Pouilly-Locheé poo-yee low-shay		
Fuissé fwee-say	Pouilly-Vinzelles poo-yee vanh-zell		
Chaintré shan-tray			
Vergisson vaire-gee-sawn			

BURGUNDY Beaujolais

Moulin-à-Vent moo-lan ah vawn	Le Moulin-à-Vent La Rochelle la row-shell Les Chants-de-cour lay shan-duh-koor	fresh, fruity, charming, young, agreeable	stews, hearty vegetable soup, omelettes, pot roast, Gruyère, Chèvre
Fleurie flur-ree	Clos de la Roilette cloh duh la rawh-let		
Saint-Amour san amoor	Champs-Grillés shan gree-yea		
Juliénas jule-yea-nahs	Les Mouilles lay moo-ye		
	Château des Capitans shot-toe day cap-e-tahn		

28

Chablis	Vaudésir	fleeting	oysters,
shab-lee	vo-day-zeer	bouquet, dry,	clam,
	Les Clos	clean,	cold fowl,
	lay cloh	flinty	Appenzeller
	Grenouilles		
	gre-noo-eyuh		
	Valmur		
	val-mewr		
	Preuses		
	proozuh		
	Bougros		
	boo-gro		
	Les Fôrets		
	lay foe-ray		
Fyé	Blanchots		
fie-yea	blawn-sho		

There are many great wines in Burgundy, and this list, of course, does not mention all of them. For example, on the Côte de Nuits, 419 vineyard names are officially acknowledged as Burgundian *climats*, with more than double that amount for the Côte de Beaune. And while the two subsections comprise only one of the five wine districts of Burgundy, the Côte d'Or undisputedly produces Burgundy's greatest wines.

29

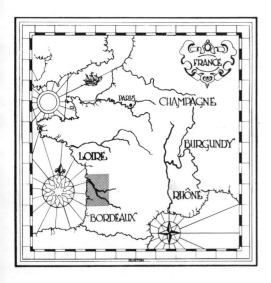

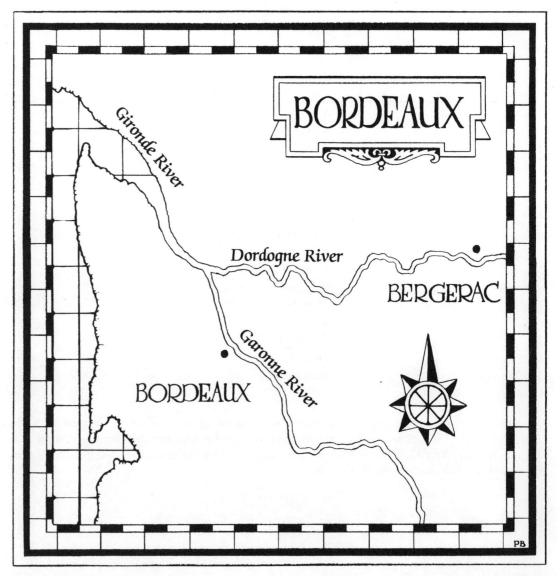

BORDEAUX

Gironde River

Dordogne River

BERGERAC

Garonne River

BORDEAUX

Bordeaux

I n ancient Roman Aquitaine — later France's historic provinces of Gascony and Guyenne — now rest the vineyards of Bordeaux. There are five distinguished wine districts: Médoc, Graves, Saint-Emilion and Pomerol, and Sauternes. This bountiful land was home to gallant, white-plumed Cyrano de Bergerac; to the Renaissance essayist Montaigne who served two terms as mayor of Bordeaux; to swashbuckling d'Artagnan, captain of the King's Musketeers; and to Montesquieu, who invented the idea of balancing powers between branches of government.

Red Bordeaux wines have the distinct characteristics of firmness, unique bouquet, lightness yet strength, and they are flowery. Different districts exemplify these as well as other characteristics in both the red and white wine, and since Bordeaux produces more than twice as much wine as Burgundy, there's plenty of room for diversification. Still, the best wine should come from acres entitled to *Appellation Contrôlée*, control laws that guarantee the place of origin and the quality standards it represents. In France, out of close to 3,000,000 acres of planted vines, less than one-fourth (about 680,000 acres) produce wines entitled to

Appellation Contrôlée. Great wines are determined by the types of soil, grapes, climate and the winemaker.

Of Bordeaux wines it is said the reds of Saint-Emilion and Pomerol most resemble full-bodied burgundies; white Graves is light and dry while the reds are rounded, sturdy and slow-maturing; Sauternes is synonymous with the greatest sweet, white wine in the world; and, the Médoc produces the most elegant, subtle yet vigorous, velvety red wine of all. The four most famous communes of Médoc, specifically the Haut-Médoc (Bordeaux's equivalent to Burgundy's Côte d'Or), are Margaux, Saint-Julien, Pauillac and Saint-Estèphe. Other towns highly ranked for their wine are Cantenac, Labarde and St. Laurent.

The debate between Burgundians and the Bordelais over which region produces the best wine will continue, no doubt, even though their circumstances differ so markedly. For instance, a large estate in Bordeaux makes wine from many grape varieties[1] but by only one person; however, Burgundy's small *climats* are planted in just one grape but each of the multiple owners makes a wine. In this way the Clos de Vougeot has 66 interpretations — a wine

---

1. (Cabernet Sauvignon, Cabernet Franc, the Carménère, Merlot, Malbec, Petit-Verdot for the reds; Sémillon, Sauvignon Blanc and Muscadelle for the whites.)

from each of its 66 owners. If the Clos de Vougeot were in Bordeaux, the cellar master (*maître de chais*) would make one wine from the 125 acres.

Moreover, the Bordelais are considered johnny-come-latelies in the wine business by the Burgundians, whose ubiquitous vines were first planted 2500 years ago. By 809 A.D., when Charlemagne was improving wine production by passing regulations — one precluded stomping grapes to press them since he thought the practice unsanitary — the Médoc was still one big marsh. The famous Bordeaux estates of today first arose during the 17th century.

Nonetheless, the Bordelais are quick to point out that Saint Emilion is considered the oldest wine town in France, stressing that the Druids (Celtic priests) used the hearty wine to celebrate their wild religious festivals. It is also claimed that Saint Emilion's Château Ausone and its vineyards cover the ancient site of a Roman villa — one belonging to its renowned namesake, Ausonius, a 4th-century man of letters. The creative poet may have been among the first to think of endorsement as a promotional device. In his memorial verses and works of prose, Ausonius wrote that Saint Emilion was the favorite wine of Julius Caesar, and the famous have been used to endorse wines ever since.

Other châteaux of St. Emilion — Château Cheval Blanc, Château Belair, Château Figeac, Château Canon — contend they produce wines that outshine the famous Ausone; and, there's no question that a glass of any of these hearty, generous reds will be rewarding. As with all outstanding wines, the more definitive the label, the better the wine should be. For example, the name of the château or vineyard is more limiting than the district (St. Emilion) which is more limiting than the region (Bordeaux). Labels of great wines include all this information and more.

It's natural for châteaux to argue about their classifications; however, there is no dispute about the significant role the British played in the Bordeaux wine trade. It all began with Eleanor of Aquitaine — a lady accustomed to the intellectual repartee and joie de vivre of the provincial Court at Bordeaux. Unfortunately, she married the rather dull and plodding Louis VII of France. Eleanor was in every respect a queen, for her training had imbued her with grace and intelligence. Still, she "absorbed all the culture and character of that free and sunny clime (Bordeaux): vigor of body and poetry of motion, passion of temper and flesh, freedom of mind and manners and speech . . . a boundless love of love and war and every pleasure."[2] Poor Louis VII was an impossible match. Eventually, Eleanor misbehaved, permitting herself a few amours (including a dashing Saracen slave) and finally obtained a divorce in 1152.

Returning happily to Bordeaux and the pleasures of its court, Eleanor was inundated with suitors. Notwithstanding her electric personality; property and possessions made her

2. Will Durant: *The Age of Faith*, chapter XXX, page 827.

dowry irrepressibly desirable. Later that season, in her thirtieth year she chose the nineteen-year-old Count of Anjou and Duke of Normandy, Henry Plantagenet, married him and eventually became the Queen of England. Casks of Bordeaux have been crossing the channel ever since.

Of the five Bordeaux wine districts, if St. Emilion were the eldest then Graves (from its gravelly soil) was the first to gain prominence. The region surrounds the city of Bordeaux, and the proximity of its vineyards to this inland port made its wines most excessible. By far the largest portion of them was shipped to England, so much so that during the Middle Ages Bretons thought Graves *was* Bordeaux. The most famous wine came from the vineyards of Haut-Brion (O-Bree-ohn). The local boys — Locke, Dryden, Bunyan and such — drank Haut-Brion in English taverns while Pepys praised it highly for all of them. The full-bodied wine appealed to the literary. By 1600 all red bordeaux was called claret, whereas before 1600 the name applied to yellowish or light red colored wines (OED) and was the British mispronunciation for *clairet*, the French word for blended red and white wines. In Samuel Johnson's 1755 dictionary he defines claret: "French wine, of a clear pale-red colour." A few years later in *Boswell* he wrote: "A man may choose between abstemiousness and knowledge, or claret and ignorance."

Haut-Brion has had an estimated 25 owners since the 16th century, but one wily diplomat deserves mention — Talleyrand. A man of varied careers, he acquired Château Haut-Brion for a few years after the French Revolution and used its precious beverage to help re-shape Europe. A government official and ally of Napoleon during the Consulate and the Empire, political differences separated them in 1812. Talleyrand was instrumental in restoring the Bourbon monarchy and in 1814 Louis XVIII gratefully made him foreign minister. In that capacity, Talleyrand achieved his greatest diplomatic triumph at the Congress of Vienna. Historically, that international conference was one of Europe's most important events and the honor of obtaining for a defeated France an equal voice among the negotiating powers goes to Monsieur Talleyrand. At intimate dinners orchestrated by the chef he shared with Czar Alexander I, (one of the delegates) he combined skill and cunning with the remarkable Haut-Brion to instill his principle of "legitimacy," defining Europe by its pre-revolutionary status. France could have been made to suffer, but the geographical decision was a victory for her. Between Talleyrand and Haut-Brion, it was accomplished.

Other excellent vineyards in Graves which produce red and white wine are Domaine de Chevalier, Château Bouscant, Château Olivier, and Château Carbonnieux. The last château was an expression of affection by 16th-century King Henry III — the peculiar, pale, damaged offspring of a diseased ancestry. He was toothless and white-haired by age 36, but he loved nothing better than adorning himself with pearls and jewels and all feminine finery, and he spent lavishly on his favorite male friends. One such gesture was the construction of a hunting lodge for Duc d'Epernon, a darling of his, and the major portion of the existing Château Carbonnieux is that dandy hunting lodge. In this preferred white wine retreat, rumor reports, the King's social trappings and transvestite tendencies were less of a travesty. The populace thought him quite mad.

Another *pieds-à-terre* of the Duc was the beautiful riverside Château Beychevelle, known in his day, the 16th century, as Brassier. After his appointment as Grand Admiral of France, so they say, the ships sailing past Beychevelle would *baisser les voiles,* (lower their sails). The tipping of the sails to salute the Admiral and the tipsy state of the sailors in calling the command eventually named the place.

Myth has it that the usually relaxed Saint Vincent appeared tipsy and disturbed, but not mad, when he had to leave his beloved *vignoble,* especially the great reds of Château La Mission-Haut-Brion. It seems that the patron saint of vintners had been summoned to that "far better place upstairs," and worse yet, unsatiated by French wines. He languished for sometime, hoping the angels and archangels or some celestial being would take pity, for he longed to romp once again with the joys that flowed from the vineyards. Finally, his gloomy state gained attention and the powerful fellows in the great beyond learned of his desire, and, relenting, gave him a leave of absence to imbibe upon his promise to return. He gave it and left hurriedly. Several weeks later he had not returned and the scouts went searching. Realizing his penchant for the reds of Château La Mission-Haut-Brion, they headed straight for that property. From the area of the wine storage sheds (*chais*) came the juiciest sounds of a happy drunk, and sure enough, that's where they found Saint Vincent, irreparably intoxicated and unfit for travel. Enraged by such an unbecoming display, the Saint was turned to stone immediately, and there he sits today, they say of his statue. With a precarious tilt on his ecclesiastical hat and a slight grin about his puffy eyes, Saint Vincent rests blessedly, forever among the great vineyards of France.

Vineyard owner, author and wine expert Alexis Lichine defined a great wine as "one that is true to type, excellent year after year, and long-lived. A wine has characteristics that take years to develop (balance, bouquet and finesse are three), and if it doesn't live to reach its prime, it is not considered great." (Alexis Lichine, *Wines of France*; p. 14.)

For those who prefer the great clarets above all wines, the Médoc is worshipped for its progeny. In this land of gravel, previously a marsh reclaimed by a 17th century Dutchman, the red wines reach the sort of perfection which has distinguished them for more than 200 years.

Since 1855, when 61 wines from Médoc and Graves were classified for the International Exhibition in Paris, Château Lafite-Rothschild has occupied the number one position. The reds were listed according to merit (based on price) and placed in five categories called *crus* (the French term for growth, production of wine or vine-estate). Every wine proprietor felt entitled to *premiers crus,* thinking anything less than first-rate must be second-rate. Nothing could have been further from the truth. All the wines were considered exceptional. Then, of course, there were other contentions. With the exception of Graves, whose Haut-Brion was listed, the reds of St. Emilion and Pomerol were ignored. St. Emilion and Graves received official classification during the 1950's; Pomerol had none; and, Alexis Lichine gave Médoc a revised listing in 1962, but he also mentioned 190 Bordeaux reds that included Graves, Pomerol and St. Emilion. Apart from the top name on the list, no true son of Gascony would dare agree with it, and so, classification contests are destined to be ongoing.

Certainly Baron James de Rothschild, who purchased Lafite in 1868, or his descendants would have no quarrel with the classification. The name itself (Lafite) derives from variations on an old Médoc word *(lahite)* meaning height. And any wine which has maintained a number one ranking for 116 years has to be reckoned by even the most skeptical as the *ne plus ultra* of the vine.

From earlier times, Lafite was the chosen claret of Louis Francois, Duc de Richelieu, King Louis XV's governor of Guyenne. Richelieu's innumerable amorous adventures were legendary. As a matter of fact, he was the champion adulterer of his era. The 18th-century aristocracy didn't frown at these encounters; indeed, adultery was much more acceptable than divorce. *C'est la vie.* Well, the old reprobate lived to such a lusty old age with such vigor that King Louis asked him how he managed it all so well. Richelieu was quick to reply with one word: Lafite.

After Eleanor captured Henry's heart, the Bretons were in Aquitaine (Bordeaux's ancient province called Guyenne in Richelieu's time) for 300 years. Actually, the Bordelais liked British rule because their kings seldom came to Gascony (part of Aquitaine) and the independent Gascons could fairly well run the show themselves. In addition, the English boosted the wine trade with their consumption, favorable taxes and concessions. Of course, it was not altogether an even matter. There were ups and downs, especially during the Hundred Years' War. It began when France's King Charles IV died without a son. Edward III, King of England, claimed the French crown. Through a series of royal marriages, he said, he had become the most direct descendant of the Capetian dynasty. "Ha!" the French said. They weren't about to have a British king.

The Bordelais, however, had a different perspective from the rest of their countrymen, and their loyalties were mixed. In any event, the war ended in 1453 with the Bordelais supporting the British in a battle led by John Talbot, the Earl of Shrewsbury. Château Talbot commemorates the commander, for he was especially admired on two accounts. The old soldier was at least 80-years-old the day of the final siege and, because of a previous promise to the French King who had released him after capture, he refused to use his sword against France. Allegedly, this last battle involved another château, unfortunately one that was almost destroyed during the fighting. Only one relic does remain: it is the old stone, towered gateway that escaped the fire and now appears on the label of Château Latour.

As with many wine properties in the Médoc, the Latour estate shares a border with the Gironde River. In the 12th century, a series of fortifications existed along the landside as protection against pirates. The famous Latour tower formed one of the masonary blockhouses that relayed the defense along the shore. And while these early owners were thought to be pro-Plantagenet, they were not opposed to accepting tribute equally from the British and the Bordelais, who no doubt welcomed the protection.

Today the major interest of Château Latour is still pro-Plantagenet, or at least it is held by an English company that represents British Viscount Cowdray. The 1962 purchase was not all smooth sailing either. A number of Frenchmen thought that a first growth (*premiers crus)* of such great fame should not be acquired by foreigners, even though someone remarked that Americans owned Château Haut-Brion (first growth) as well as Château Lascombes (second growth).

The alarm having been sounded, General de Gaulle was consulted and made a remark that purportedly solved the matter: "An English company can scarcely remove French soil."

Another Britisher, Robert Walpole — the English statesman often called Britain's first prime minister — was a friend of France. And he definitely admired French wine. The records of John Hervey, first Earl of Bristol and lord of the privy seal, show that Walpole bought four hogsheads (63 gal. barrels) of Château Margaux regularly throughout the year of 1732. He entertained luxuriously at his home in Norfolk as well as in London, spending £ 1,118 annually on wine. That amount is roughly the equivalent of $59,000 today. Well, it seems Mr. Walpole wanted to make London a free port, and with such an enormous wine bill, it's certainly understandable. Something was definitely in order. In any event, the notion of free trade may be attributable, at least in part, to Robert Walpole's sizable thirst for Château Margaux.

In a region that produces abundant excellent wine, only five châteaux have been classified in the coveted first growth category: Lafite, Margaux, Latour, Haut-Brion and Mouton. These châteaux share another common factor. Just as many of the large estates that developed during the 18th century, their money came from the new aristocracy, the *noblesse de robe*. The families owed their acquired prestige to the Bordeaux Parlement, a court of justice. As the old aristocracy gradually declined in the 17th century, it was slowly replaced by rich merchants and men acquiring rank from positions in the Parlement. Prerequisites for membership in this select club were money and catholicity. The major offices, such as president, were appointed by the crown, but other members claimed nobility because the Parlementaires might judge them and nobles were entitled to be tried by their peers. Rather far-fetched, but apparently it worked. In any event, the earliest families connected with these distinguished growths were the legal men of the *noblesse de robe*.

Many of them acquired their wealth through tenants who rented and worked the vineyard as share croppers. When the tenant owed money, for whatever reason, the seigneur withheld his share. Or if a peasant owned a patch and had financial problems, the land was taken and he was thrown off of it. It is not surprising that some of the *noblesse* were led to the guillotine at the end of the century.

Others, however, became fabulously wealthy and, conveniently, died before the Revolution. For instance, the Marquis de Ségur, a president of the Parlement, was called *le prince des vignes*. At one time before his death in 1755, he owned Latour, Lafite, and Mouton as well as other property.

Baron Nathaniel de Rothschild purchased Mouton in 1835, but it was the dedication, perseverance and hard work of his great-grandson, Philippe, who made Mouton one of Bordeaux's top five clarets. Its original 1855 listing as a second growth constitutes the longest, most controversial wine classification in Bordeaux history. After an effort of twenty years, Baron Philippe de Rothschild accomplished the reclassification of Château Mouton-Rothschild as a first growth. *Voila!*

As the smallest of Bordeaux's claret districts, Pomerol was part of Saint Emilion until 1923. Size apart, one of a great Pomerol's most distinctive characteristics is *le vin a du nez,* great nose, the term applied when a wine has a tremendous, rich bouquet. In this sense, the wine is as big as the nose of Cyrano, who said: "a great nose indicates a great man — genial, courteous, intellectual, virile and courageous," substituting wine for man, of course.

Perhaps that overstates the case a bit, but Pomerol has a certain finesse that makes it almost as appealing as Cyrano. Among its many estates, Château Pétrus is the best known, albeit, modest. Small is also delicious in Bordeaux, where château means a wine estate, not a magnificent castle. The property usually surrounds a country house which may indeed look like a palace or be simply a farmhouse or something in between. Château-bottled wine is made and bottled on the estate where the vineyards and wine-making are under the direction of the owner. Château La Conseillante, Château l'Evangile, Château Trotanoy, Château La Fleur Pétrus and Château Vieux-Château-Certan are among the many fine producers of Pomerol.

Bordeaux clarets are famous, but Sauternes is unique not only among Bordeaux but of all French wines. To begin with, grapes for Sauternes (last "s" silent) are picked individually, not clipped in bunches, and only as each grape reaches its perfect moment of read-iness. Rows are picked as much as ten times for two or more months (most grape harvests take about ten days). The harvest occurs exceptionally late in autumn to permit an im-portant mold (*pourriture noble*) to influence the sugar and alcohol content, the grape con-centrate and the amount of glycerine that make Sauternes so special. It is a rich, entirely natural, white, sweet wine from only the Sauternes region in France. (In the United States, the name Sauternes is used as freely as Chablis to mean almost any white wine.) One French oenophile of the French Acadamy of Wine described the genuine article as "the most sumptuous of those white wines that are strictly natural: unctuous, velvety, li-querish, highly perfumed, with a great strength that is, however, fine, elegant, and filled with nuances." One vine makes one glassful.

Representing the greatest excellence of this unique wine is Château d'Yquem. Just as the Graves and Médoc clarets, it was selected as a first growth in the 1855 classification, the only other Bordeaux district to be so gratified. Shortly before that time, the Czar's brother, Grand Duke Constantine, paid 20,000 francs for a cask of d'Yquem (approximately $30,000 on today's market). Another Russian noble found the 1868 d'Yquem irresistible. In those days, and until fairly recent times, wine expert Edmund Penning-Rowsell says wine was shipped in cask and without labels, which were probably supplied by the importer and bottler. In any event, the extravagant Moscow resident insisted that his Sauternes be placed in cut-glass decanters with the appropriate golden engravings, Château d'Yquem, vintage year.

What a fantastic way to end a story. And how fitting that it should end with a dessert wine.

The estimated number of vineyards in Bordeaux is 1000. Many have a great château and considerable acres of vines and bottle their wine. Many more have small farm houses and make regional wine. It would be impossible to list all the fine Bordeaux wines here. Such lists are readily available in other wine books. The intention of *Vin Vignettes* is to make the reader familiar and comfortable with wines and pique interest.

BORDEAUX (Médoc) clarets

Commune	Château (wine-estate)	General characteristics	Food suggestions
Pauillac paw-yak	Château Lafite-Rothschild shah-toe la-feet rowht-sheeld Château Mouton-Rothschild Château mootohn rowht-sheeld Château Latour Château lahtour Château Lynch-Bages Château lanshuh baajuh Château Pichon-Longueville Château pea-shohn lown-guh-veal	subtle yet vigorous, elegant, long lived, delicate, finesse, balanced, full bouquet (Médocs need at least ten years to mature)	beef and lamb, Roquefort, Brie, roast beef, rack of lamb, stews beef and lamb, Gorgonzola, Gruyère, Coulommiers
Margaux mar-go	Château Margaux Château mar-go Château Lascombes Château lah caumb Château Rausan-Ségla Château roe-sahn segg-la Château Palmer Château paul-mare	silky, soft, perfumed bouquet	beef, veal and roast fowl, Stilton, Camembert, Emmenthal

BORDEAUX (Médoc) clarets

Commune	Château (wine-estate)	General characteristics	Food suggestions
Saint Julien sant shoo-lee-anh	Château Talbot Château tal-bow Château Beychevelle Château bayshuh-vel Château Gruaud-Larose Château grew-o lah-rohsuh Château Léoville Las Cases Château lay-o-veal lahs cahss	soft, charming, elegant wine, full-bodied	roasted poultry, lamb, sweetbreads, Brie
Saint-Estèphe san tas-tef	Château Calon-Ségur Château cal-awhn segguhr Château Cos-d'Estournel Château cause des-toor-nel Château Montrose Château mahn-rohse	big, robust, long-lived, assertive, sturdy, body	game, aged beef, Roquefort, Camembert

48

Saint Emilion and Pomerol clarets

Saint Emilion sant a-me-lee-awhn	Château Ausone shah-toe ozone Château Cheval Blanc Château shev-val blanh Château Belair Château bell-air Château Figeac Château fee-jak Château Canon Château can-awhn	mature earlier than Médocs, full, round, smooth, hearty	beef, veal, fowl, Cheddars, Port-Salut
Pomerol paum-mae-rawhl	Château Pétrus Château pay-truss Château La Conseillante Château la con-say-yahnt Château l'Evangile Château leh-vah-geel Château Vieux-Château- Certan Château vee-uh Château saire- tohn	big nose, full-bodied, soft, mature early, intense aroma and flavor	beef, veal and fowl, Roquefort, Brie Pont-l'Evêque

Graves, white and reds

Pessac pess-sak	Château La Mission-Haut-Brion (red) Château la me-see-awhn o-bree-ohn	full, considerable breed, rounded	beef and lamb, with reds Bleu d'Auvergne
	Château Haut-Brion Château o bree-ohn	full-bodied, sturdy, holding quality, mellows with age	game, beef and lamb, Roquefort
Cadaujac caw-dozak	Château Bouscant Château boose-cahn		fowl, ham and seafood with whites
Léognan lay-own-yahw	Château Carbonnieux Château car-bahn-yuh Château Olivier, Château o-leev-ee-a	pale, dry, light whites	Edam, Gouda, Feta

Sauternes, whites

Sauternes saw-tern	Château d'Yquem Château dee kim Château Climens Château clee-mah Château Coutet Château coo-tay Château Suduirant Château sued-wee-row Château Filhot Château fee-oh	rich, golden, sweet, high in alcohol, extraordinary fruit and breed	desserts Roquefort Camembert Grièges (Pipo Crem', in U.S.)

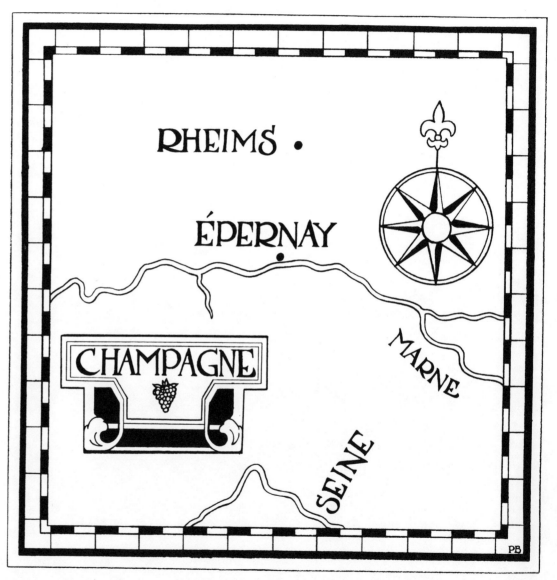

Champagne

henever you pop the cork on a bottle of champagne, you'll be in excellent company and part of a grand tradition. Some of history's most famous and glamorous personages have been addicted to the noble wine, which, more than any other, has been associated with emperors, queens, and aristocrats.

By strictest definition, champagne is that sparkling wine produced *only* in Champagne, an ancient French province 90 miles northeast of Paris. Wine has been made there since Julius Caesar conquered Gaul, but in his day it was a still wine and very different indeed. It wasn't until the 17th century that sparkling wine became a reality. According to legend, a blind Benedictine monk named Dom Pérignon discovered champagne. The year was 1690. What he experienced was the magical effects of a second fermentation. Because Champagne was (and is) the northernmost wine-producing area of France, the early advent of winter stopped fermentation prematurely. Later, after the wine was bottled, the arrival of warm spring weather created a second fermentation.

Dom Pérignon couldn't see what was happening, but he could certainly taste it. "Come quickly!" he exclaimed after his first sip. "I am drinking the stars!" This monk, whose name would be given to one of the most celebrated champagnes in the world, was also the first to use cork for stoppers. In addition, he originated blending wines of different growths, a practice that enhances the character and bouquet of champagne. For this reason, however, and unlike other French wines, it is more important to check the label for the name of the champagne firm than for vineyards; for example, Moët & Chandon, Pol Roger, Mumm, Perrier-Jouet, Krug and so forth.

Since its earliest days, Champagne has been one of the most famous of the great wine regions of France. Its sparkling wine has been called the "exquisite ambassador of French perfection," the traditional accompaniment to celebrate weddings, successes, christenings and engagements. No other wine, French or otherwise, enjoys the respect, the acclaim, and the following of champagne; and, rightly so. The delight which is synonymous with festive and great occasions had its advent at the French Court.

Champagne's debut occurred at the Palais Royal during the Regency (1715–23), an incomparably frivolous and decadent period in French history. The son and grandson of Louis XIV had died in 1711 and 1712 respectively, so upon the demise of the Sun King in 1715, only his five-year-old great-grandson was left to inherit the throne. Since the child was too young to assume full power, it was temporarily vested in a regent, the libertine Philippe, Duc d'Orleans. Excess and extravagance were the order of the day and hundreds of bottles of champagne delighted the company whose *petit soupers* scandalized Paris.

When Louis XV attained his majority and moved the Court to Versailles it proved equally as extravagant but considerably more civilized. Some historians give credit for the improvement to Madame de Pompadour, the King's remarkable, accomplished and charming mistress. Her tastes apparently set the standard of the time. She admired Voltaire: he was the rage. She valued Sévres porcelains and they became a must in all important houses. Her preference for champagne made it essential, the unquestioned royal beverage: "Give me champagne," she said. "Champagne is the only wine which leaves the beauty of a woman unblemished."

While aristocrats made de Pompadour's middle-class origin the bane of her life, few denied her breathtaking beauty, quick wit, and intelligence. In addition, she could draw, engrave, play the harpsichord, sing, dance and act: "her voice in itself was a seduction." She restored poor, bored Louis by her many ingenious entertainments. The elegant women who graced the Court of the mid-1700s modeled themselves after Madame. Their fabulous silk and satin and taffeta gowns nearly begged to be reproduced on Boucher's carefree, pink pastel canvases. The ladies danced at the lavish Court diversions and toasted Dom Pérignon to Rameau's compositions and measured the success of the fête with corks. Only the finest was suitable for such influential figures, so naturally, the elixir was champagne. It was the wine of royalty, first in France and eventually around the world.

Champagne's early association with nobility is understandable. Scarcity and cost have always enhanced prestige, and champagne was both rare and expensive. The reason is simple: champagne's sparkle occurs in the bottle during a second fermentation. It took over a century for glass makers to perfect bottles strong enough to withstand the pressure of containing the wine's effervescence. Explosions were so constant in the *caves* during the 18th century that cellar workers were issued iron masks. Even so, the *chef de cave* of a notable 19th-century house, Besserat de Bellefon, almost donated an eye. While breakage of one-tenth of the fermenting stock was thought normal, it wasn't unusual to lose three or four times that amount. Consequently, the remaining champagne was precious and costly and only aristocrats could afford it.

As conditions improved and the vogue increased, new champagne houses were founded: Clicquot, Roederer, Lanson and Heidsieck. They challenged the older firms — Ruinart, Fourneaux (now Taittinger), and Moët & Chandon — but the growing popularity of the wine insured each firm a lucrative business. Laws and taxes on wine gradually improved and foreign markets became established. Lord Chesterfield of England, modestly described as a statesman and man of letters, was the lord high steward for King George II's household. Considered the most accomplished connoisseur of food and wine of his day (1730), this most perfect host once bellowed shamelessly:

"Give me Champaign, and fill it to the brim,
  I'll toast in bumpers ev'ry lovely limb."

Long before that time, however, Champagne was a center of attention. Beginning in 816 A.D. with the son of Charlemagne (Louis the Pious), the highly decorative, full-dress coronation of French kings has taken place in Champagne's ancient Cathedral of Reims. Nonetheless, it took forty crownings, a blind monk and 884 years to toast the event with sparkling wine: *"Vive le roi! Vive la France!"* Alas, the French Revolution put an end to such goings-on, at least temporarily. But even the Revolution, which symbolized hatred of luxury and the *ancien regime,* couldn't daunt the impact of sparkling wine. Comte de Mirabeau, the most important revolutionary leader of 1792-93, had a close relative whom publications caricatured as a cask with bottle legs because he drank so much champagne; and it was rumored even Mirabeau partook. The contradictory Georges Jacques Danton, president of the Jacobin Club (a most radical revolutionary group), sympathized with the plight of the common man while he extravagantly bathed in the royal wine. When the political tables turned, Danton's compatriot, Camille Desmoulins, sang praises to the champagne of Ay (an important champagne village pronounced *eye-ee*) all the way to the guillotine.

Just after the turn of the century, Napoleon helped immortalize France's royal drink. He befriended a devoted subject, Jean-Remy Moët (mayor of Epernay) and the relationship that developed was mutually advantageous. Epernay, center of the champagne industry and home of the extensive Moët cellars, was situated along the most direct route from Paris to Germany, Poland, and Russia. Napoleon marched through Epernay regularly and the admiring and admirable Jean-Remy constructed two houses for the Emperor's Court. There was always ample champagne for the entourage, including Napoleon's armies. His troops celebrated every victory with sparkling wine, and not only did the soldier class become aware of it, but they spread its fame among their foreign adversaries. Shortly before one of his last battles, the Emperor gave his host a special tribute. He presented Mayor Moët his own Chevalier's cross of the Legion of Honor: "I want to reward you for the admirable way you have built up your business and all that you have done for our wines abroad. . . . Don't thank me. I give you what you deserve."

After the defeat of Napoleon at the Battle of Leipzig, he had to abdicate and retire to the island of Elba. The Russians then invaded France. The troops of the Czar occupied Champagne, and, finding they liked sparkling wine as well as Russian vodka, robbed the great cellars of thousands and thousands of bottles.

The Russians were not the only ones to discover champagne, of course. An ironic byproduct of the Napoleonic Wars was the spreading renown of the exceptional drink. There followed an unprecedented and overwhelming demand for the sparkling wine. For example, in 1785, firms sold 300,000 bottles. But by 1844, six and a half million bottles were purchased and four million of them went abroad. By 1900, sales approximated 30 million bottles, and the 1909 figure was 39 million.

There has been a good bit of speculation about what caused such phenomenal growth: the relative peace over those years, the prosperity brought about by the Industrial Revolution, better transportation, the good business sense of the champagne makers. One theory gives credit to Britain, attributing champagne's success to the Naughty Nineties and the Edwardian Era. In any event, more wine became available as new firms were created: Perrier (1825), Mumm (1827), Bollinger (1829), Pommery & Greno and Deutz & Geldermann (1836), Krug (1843) and Pol Roger (1849).

Pol Roger exported more champagne to England between the World Wars than any of the firms. Sir Winston Churchill preferred it above all others and even named one of his racing horses "Pol Roger." And as Britishers were toasting their beloved Queen Elizabeth the day she was crowned in 1953, "Pol Roger" won the Black Prince Stakes Handicap at Kempton. After Sir Winston died in 1965, the firm's owners added a black border to the label to honor the Prime Minister. At another royal occasion some 28 years later, Prince Charles and his new bride, Princess Diana, joined 120 family members for the wedding breakfast where an orchestra serenaded the couple as the guests toasted the bride and groom with Krug champagne and dined on *Suprême de Volaille Princesse de Galles* (chicken breasts stuffed with lamb mousse).

To evidence that Champagne ladies are often exceptional, the House of Krug has a story about a remarkable Madame Krug, grandmother of today's proprietors — Henri and Remi. Their champagne has been made only by male family members for five generations, men who have blended only white wines made from Chardonnay grapes since 1843 — with one diversion. During World War I Joseph Krug II was taken prisoner. Jeanne Krug Hollier-Larousse, his wife, assumed the operation and stubbornly remained in Reims, a city paralyzed by relentless artillery shells. The bombardments prohibited transporting white grapes from the Côtes des Blancs, so Madame Krug broke tradition by using Pinot Noir (black grapes) from the nearby Montagne de Reims. When Joseph learned of it, he feared the worst for the purity of his family's champagne style. However, the 1915 vintage was acclaimed one of Krug's best; a success that would have pleased Madame's champagne drinking godfather — Victor Hugo.

Meanwhile, the American market was understandably slower to develop. Sea voyages were not pleasant for passengers or the wine. One early account records the miserable and risky Atlantic crossing made in 1832 by Edmond Ruinart. In those days the head of the firm rather than an agent sold his own champagne so the contacts were likely to be important. In this instance Edmond Ruinart visited President Andrew Jackson at the White House to give him a case of Ruinart Champagne. It was a gracious gesture, graciously received.

Relations, unfortunately, weren't always that cordial. Once the international markets for champagne were established, other countries, such as Germany, Spain and the United States, began to manufacture their own versions of the sparkling wine. That fact didn't bother the Champenois. They realized they couldn't produce sufficient quantities to satisfy the world market. What did enrage them, however, was the dishonest practice of trying to pass foreign sparkling wine for French champagne. Most of these countries eventually desisted. They conceded, by treaty or trade arrangement, that champagne is an appellation of origin and rightfully belongs to the progeny of their Gallic ancestors. So they adopted other names for their sparkling wines: *sekt* (Germany), *espumosa* (Spain), *spumante* (Italy), and even in France the sparkling wine not produced in Champagne is called *vin mousseux*.

One exception has been the United States. Many American winemakers continued — and continue today — to call their sparkling wine champagne. In the 1880s, a town in New York was even renamed Rheims (the French dropped the "h" 200 years ago and pronounce it "Rrr-anz") and an older French woman with the propitious name of Madame Veuve Pommery was imported to found the wine company.

The incident provoked repercussions. For more than 25 years during the early part of this century, the *Appellation d'Origine Contrôlée* laws were being developed in France. A separate clause dealing with the champagne processes defined the *méthode champenoise,* making champagne the most rigorously controlled and carefully made wine in the world. Nonetheless, a number of American winemakers still call their sparkling wine champagne.

In 1913, three million bottles of champagne were exported to the United States. But those days were followed by Prohibition and the Crash. Hard times were experienced around the world. After World War II the United States emerged with a prosperous economy and a population willing to spend more money to have real French champagne. Many American soldiers experienced champagne for the first time when General George Patton marched his victorious troops into Epernay (a memorial near the train station honors them). The Champenois opened their cellars to them, deliriously grateful.

In 1981, France exported almost eight million bottles of champagne to the United States. It was used to launch everything from ships to debutantes and a good deal in between, but it is definitely no longer reserved for the aristocracy. Indeed, with a little planning, almost anyone can celebrate an event with the special delights of a bottle of champagne. It is the one wine that is appropriate before, during, and after a meal — or served as a festive beverage on any occasion.

FRENCH CHAMPAGNE FIRMS

Moët & Chandon
(moo-ette eh shan-dohn)

Pol Roger
(pole row-jay)

Charles Heidsieck
(charwl ed-sick)

Lanson
(lahn-sawn)

Krug
(khrr oog)

de Meric
(duh Mair-eek)

Bollinger
(bowl-en-jay)

Philipponnat
(fee-lip-po-nah)

Perrier-Jouet
(pear-re-a jou-ette)

Dom Ruinart
(dohm rue-e-nar)

Louis Roederer
(lew-ee rrow-duh-rair)

Pommery & Greno
(paum-may-ree eh gree-no)

Deutz & Geldermann
(duhtz eh gell-dair-mann)

Veuve-Cliquot
(vuhv clee-ko)

Piper Heisieck
(pea-pear ed-sick)

Mumm
(moom)

Taittinger
(tet-tahn-jay)

Besserat de Bellefon
(bess-ser-rah duh bell-fonh)

[Some of the elite, smaller manufacturers (such as *de Meric*) are available only in France at this printing.]

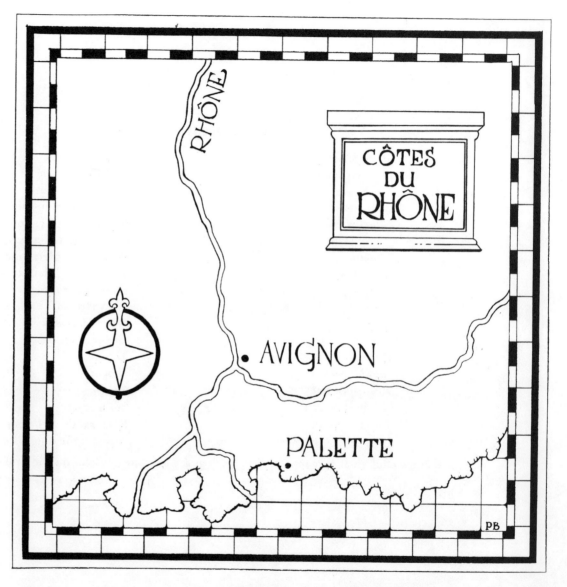

CÔTES DU RHÔNE

RHÔNE

AVIGNON

PALETTE

PB

Rhône

n 1930 Zoë Akins wrote a play titled *The Greeks Had a Word for It,* the idea being that Greeks were originators and bright enough to make impressive innovations. When some traveling Grecian traders and settlers of 600 B.C. landed in what is now Marseille (Massalia then) to found a colony, they found, in addition, that the wine in their amphorae did not ship well. With their usual initiative, they decided there was only one thing to do — make their own. And so the hills and banks along the Rhône River all the way to Switzerland now flourish with the Syrah, Grenache, and Viognier, grapes that thrive in France's hot southern clime. Ancient Greek wine — probably sweet, sometimes muddy with sediment, or mixed with honey and/ or water — bears little resemblance to modern Rhône wine. Still, in all likelihood, this area was France's first *vignoble.* In any event, it was a lucrative one. History records that the enterprising Greek merchants lived well and sponsored some of the most opulent markets of the day. By the end of the Second Punic War (218-201 B.C.) Massalia was a smashing commercial success.

Word spread and the Celts in the region paid attention. Ironmongers and warmongers with equal zeal, they introduced the Greeks to iron gardening tools which made tending the soil a breeze, but they also gave them an invention — soap — which made life more pleasant for all. In spite of promising trade relations, the Celtic disposition for war and tribute overcame them and they attacked. Some Romans happened to be in the area on their way to sack the Carthaginians, so the Greeks called for help. The rest is history. The Greeks came under Roman rule (147 B.C.) and Rome began its world domination. France, however, continued its pursuit of fine wines.

During 1150–1250, roads — such as they were — crisscrossed with various entertaining and enterprising folk. Troubadours roamed the countryside laden with the wines and songs that charmed damsels and romanced civilization into a code of chivalry that made wars seem well-mannered and illicit affairs elegant. Crusaders trudged under their heavy religious burdens, and traveling merchants, enjoying the fruits of an unrestrained trade, brought new ideas and circumstance. Heretical sects such as the abstinent Albigenses in southern France confused the religious and poetic issues with their no-shades-of-gray, good or bad dualism. All in all, it was enough to make a weary pilgrim want to retire. Indeed, that was the decision of Gaspard de Sterimberg, a product of the Middle Ages. According to legend, either wishing his "too too solid flesh would melt," or finding the "world too much with him," Gaspard headed for a lonely hill high above the Rhône River. Satisfied with an isolated spot from which he could view life below without participating in it, he planted his vines. In time there was wine, and the hermit shared it with passersby, a kindly act considering the condition of the water. It was undrinkable. Bad water made the wine even more popular and Gaspard's hermitage became famous. Apparently he made wine with all the energy of his unrequited passions, for wine experts describe the reds and whites from the vines of L'Hermitage as "the manliest of wines."

The vineyards are terraced up the steep, rocky slope that shadows the little town of Tain in its valley, perhaps 50 miles south of Lyon. Hermitage (also Ermitage) is one of France's oldest vineyards, and although the wines are harsh in their youth, the reds become big, soft and rich with age, and, of all dry whites, these need time to discard their hardness, maybe four or more years. They last well for whites, fifteen years and longer.

Ruins of Sainte-Christophe chapel supposedly mark the spot of the hermit's hut, and the two seem to have had at least one characteristic in common. It was the simplicity of both hermit and saint that appealed to the unsophisticated medieval mind. For instance, St. Christopher was allegedly eighteen feet tall, a physical fact that made fasting difficult because he had to do without so much more wine and food than most brethren. His size made him clumsy too, particularly when his bovine tongue tried to recite prayers. Anyway, having learned that kings were all-powerful, he chose to serve a king. But when he saw the royal ruler make the sign of the cross upon hearing Satan's name, Christopher decided the Devil must have more puissance and followed him. However, when they encountered a cross, the Devil ran away. In consequence, Christopher believed Jesus must be the greatest power of all, and rejoicing with sacred wine, devoted his life to Christ.

One thing neither hermit nor saint had the good fortune to enjoy was the incomparable cuisine of Fernand Point, one of the greatest chefs of modern times (1897–1955). His restaurant, La Pyramide, is named after a Roman obelisque nearby, between the vineyards and the restaurant. Even among Michelin's three star gastronomic temples, La Pyramide is considered a stellar experience. The *carte de vin* lists many Rhône wines, and the Rhône River separates La Pyramide from two of them, Côte Rôtie and Condrieu.

Rôtie is a useful word. If *beurrée* follows it, the phrase means buttered toast; put côte before rôtie and it means roasted slope. Among France's red wine vineyards, the "roasted slope" is one of the most famous. It has two sections, La Brune and La Blonde. The less romantic attribute the names to obvious differences in the two soils; iron oxide giving La Brune a brownish clay and chalk making La Blonde lighter. However, those with a troubadour's heart give their credence to a winsome tale.

In the days of noblemen, the Rhône village of Ampuis boasted a kindly lord, the generous Monsieur Maugiron. So generous, in fact, was this good sire that he gave his two daughters each a valuable vineyard. One of the girls was fair and demure, a gentle soul with refreshing youthful vivacity, but alas, she tired quickly. The older daughter was a comely, buxom lass, with dark features. When provoked, she reacted with harshness; however, if properly soothed, in time she would mellow and be soft as velvet. And so, indeed, are the wines.

The other vineyard downriver from La Pyramide is Condrieu. It produces full-bodied white wines that have the dubious distinction of being characterized with a taste called *goût de terroir* (taste of earth). Once identified, the flavor is unforgettable and unmistakable. Condrieu also contains a substantially perfumed bouquet. The wine seldom leaves France since the limited production is consumed in the district.

Another small vineyard, Château Grillet, produces even less white wine and has the smallest Appellation Contrôlée in France. Appellation Contrôlée (AC) laws dictate every matter that influences wine. The legislative intent of them is simply to protect France's fine wines and the AC considerations include: area of soil permitted production, permissible grapevines, alcoholic content, viticultural practices, permissible size of harvest, vinicultural practices, and distilling (which applies to spirits, not wines). Château Grillet, supremely dry and well-balanced, is the exceptional *vin du pays* or outstanding local wine.

It was the winegrowers of Rhône, precisely those of Avignon's Châteauneuf-du-Pape, who first passed regulations which set the pattern for Appellation Contrôlée. Convincing independent-minded French wine producers they needed regulations wasn't easy. But, Baron Le Roy de Boiseaumarié, a distinguished grower of Châteauneuf-du-Pape, began with his example and arguments in the 1900s. Laws were made, 1905, and modified, 1908, and modified, 1911, and modified, 1914, and reinterpreted, 1919, and on and on until they were finally established in 1935, but the dialogue continues.

Meanwhile, Châteauneuf-du-Pape has been doing very nicely.

Before the beginning of a religious Avignon, there had been a 230-year conspiracy (1073–1303) by the popes to forge a united theocratic Europe by subordinating all kings. When it failed, French King Philip IV, according to some, acted unduly toward his mutinous rival, Pope Boniface VIII, by arresting and half-starving the man. Apparently the irate Italians felt such malfeasance was reserved for Rome, and in consequence, France's Pope Clément V — a Frenchman who feared the worst from Italians — was crowned in Lyons and promptly moved the papal seat to Avignon (1309). That move marked the beginning of what history records as the Babylonian Captivity — a reference to the Babylonian forced exile of the Jews from Jerusalem (586 B.C.). Seven French popes ruled the Roman Catholic Church from Avignon for almost seventy years. The Italians felt it was bad enough that Clément was French, worse that he had only been a bishop of Bordeaux (where he planted the vines for Château Pape Clément). The rest of Europe wasn't too enamored with the situation either, and to add to Pope Clément's difficulties, the papacy was a virtual prisoner of the French Court. At his death, Clément passed along his sacramental wine and troubles to an aged (72 years) John XXII who served eighteen unexpected years before passing along his cap to Benedict XII. These French pontiffs came from simple backgrounds — cobblers and bakers and such. But when Clément VI, who was descended from a noble house, began his reign, he saw no sense in austerity whatsoever. He continued the construction of the huge Palace of the Popes and its conglomerate Gothic buildings and courts, ramparts and towers. Circling this compound were smaller palaces, houses and huts which held "prelates, envoys, lawyers, merchants, artists, poets, servants, soldiers, beggars and prostitutes of every grade from cultured courtesans to tavern tarts. . . . Avignon now assumed the morals as well as manners of royal court." (Will Durant; *The Renaissance*, p. 53.) Of course a summer retreat was essential and so the "New Castle" of Châteauneuf-du-Pape was constructed among the luscious vineyards some ten miles away.

All that remains of that edifice is a crumbling wall, but the vineyards are as luscious and productive as ever.

Another Avignon relic is familiar because schoolchildren around the world sing "Sur le pont, d'Avignon, l'on y danse." The bridge was built during the 12th century when the Church supported construction projects through religious fraternities, *fréres pontifs,* by indulging them with indulgences for their work. Bridges didn't form a connective network because medieval highways were dusty or muddy paths filled with potholes and commercial transport was impossible. Until the *fréres pontifs,* road maintenance was the responsibility of the man who owned land next to it and he seldom saw sense in expending money and energy for transients. Anyway, most Rhône wines stayed at home and were drunk locally.

Luckily, that is no longer the case. Almost 99% of Châteauneuf-du-Pape's production is red wine and a good amount of its annual two million gallons is shipped to the United States. The crimson, full-bodied Rhône is better known than Hermitage or Côte Rôtie, perhaps because it matures more quickly and can be enjoyed when only three years old. The Apellation Contrôlée for Châteauneuf-du-Pape requires $12^1/_2$% natural alcohol, the highest of any in France. Just as most French wines, the finest is estate-bottled from such outstanding vineyards as Château Fortia, Château des Fines-Roche, and several others.

To the west, across the river from Chateauneuf-du-Pape is the wine district of Tavel, France's best known and perhaps best tasting rosé. It was said to be the favorite wine of Francis I. As a patron of the arts, the King sponsored some notable 16th-century artists and writers and may even have shared a glass of rosé with his protégés: Cellini, da Vinci and Rabelais.

As with all wines, color is important to rosé. It should resemble a sturdy, deep pink, somewhere between tourmaline and carnelian; definitely without any hint of orange. Rosés are lighter than reds because the grape skins are in contact with the juice for a much shorter period of time. This limitation of skin-to-juice contact also decreases tannin, an organic compound which permits the wine to mature more slowly. Rosés are drunk chilled, young — under two years — and go with any menu at any meal.

RHONE

Côte Rôtie (reds) coat row-tee	ruby colored wines, violet aromas, tannic, require years to mature	game strong cheeses
Condrieu (white) cawn-dree-yuh	golden, floral wines, robust, drink young	seafood — fish and shellfish
Château Grillet (white) shah-toe gree-yaye	perfumed, spicy, dry vigorous, early maturing	fish with mild sauces
Hermitage (red/white) aire-mee-tahj	deep ruby, tannic, robust, long lived, well-balanced golden, great finesse, floral, clean	roast beef, steaks and game, Brie, fish dishes
Tavel (rosé) tah-vell	pink, fresh, clear, drink young (under 2 years)	white meats — veal, ham, poultry
Châteauneuf-du-Pape (red) shah-toe-neuf-dew-pop	rich, full-bodied, long lived, robust, potent	game and cheeses with vigor
Châteauneuf-du-Pape (white) shah-toe-neuf-dew-pop	spicy, pleasant, warm	fish

73

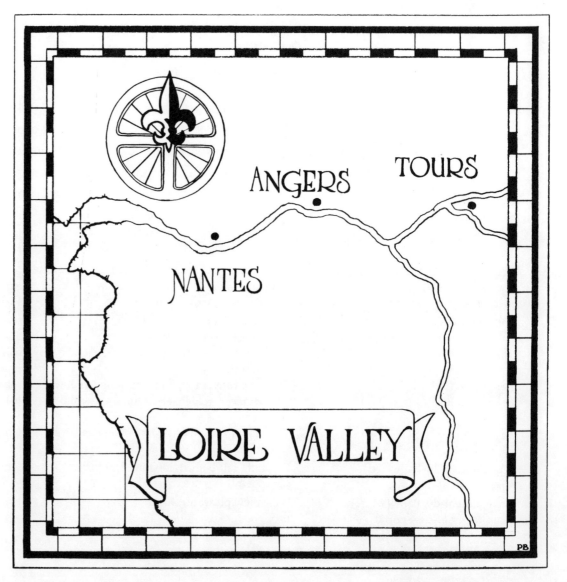

FRANCE

PARIS
CHAMPAGNE
BURGUNDY
LOIRE
RHÔNE
BORDEAUX

ANGERS

TOURS

NANTES

LOIRE VALLEY

Loire

T he Loire River treks a tiresome 634 miles to the Atlantic from its headwaters in southeastern France, as if indeed "Even the weariest river winds somewhere safe to sea" (Swinburne). From the city of Nevers westward, the Loire wine regions produce a charming variety of impressive dry and sweet whites, light reds, rosés, and even a number of sparkling renditions — one with a demi-fizzle, *pétillant,* and those with a robust sparkle second only to Champagne, *mousseux.* Most of the Loire wines are drunk in France because they are best when young and many do not have enough alcohol to travel well.

This River, the longest in France, shares a reputation with the surrounding area as the loveliest, oldest civilized, and most cultured part of France. Notwithstanding that fact, Anjou was once a frontier. The cowboys and rangers of this western land, however, were counts. When the Frankish tribes invaded Gaul, they established counts in these dangerous outposts to represent the crown, giving them instant nobility, prestige, and local autonomy in one fell swoop. Anjou and Brittany (the most unconventional province in France) were two such places, and the wine produced, Muscadet, has lived through the centuries to rival Chablis as the perfect accompaniment for the succulent treasures from the sea: lobsters, clams, shrimps, and the *Portugaise* oysters.

Muscadet was the wine drunk by Abélard, a native son of Brittany born near Nantes. He was many things; a rebel, a 12th-century scholastic philosopher, theologian, and one of the original minds behind the University of Paris.

During his day, there was a rather large dispute among theologians and philosophers that concerned nominalism versus conceptualism versus realism. Suffice it to say, Abélard perpetuated the controversy and riled the Church because its beliefs were being disavowed. In addition, he possessed the arrogance normal to an attractive and bright twenty-four-year-old (ca., 1089). "Abélard had a fine figure, a proud carriage, good looks . . . ; and the vivacity of his spirit gave charm to his manners . . . he was gay and joyous, a conceited, boastful, insolent, self-centered youth who rode with young thoughtlessness over the dogmas and sensibilities of his masters and his time." (Durant: *Age of Faith*; p. 934). These attributes did not make him popular with the canonical leaders of the old faith, and their disfavor would bring him tragedy.

Age and study helped Abélard intellectually but did nothing to quell his generous self-image. In 1115, when he was forty-one-years old, Abélard became a clergyman and established his own series of lectures in Paris's Notre Dame Cathedral School. Students flocked from Spain, England, Flanders, Germany, and of course, from France to squat at his feet. Mixing eloquence and humor, he was irresistible and earned himself a nice purse as well as international fame. One fair attendant, the teenaged Héloïse, had loved learning so well that the convent nuns declared her their brightest pupil. Her uncle, a catholic canon, was impressed by the news and sent her to Notre Dame to hear Abélard. Upon seeing Héloïse, Abélard "determined to unite himself in the bonds of love." Of course such thoughts, much less actions, would not be accepted by the cloth, but the wine flowed and love was uncontained. In time Héloïse announced to Abélard that she was with child. He wanted to marry her secretly but she feared for his ecclesiastical career. Eventually, however, they did, but the secret was kept while the pregnancy was found out and as Abélard reported: ". . . they laid a plot against me; and one night while . . . I was asleep, broke into my lodgings. There they had vengeance upon me with a most cruel and shameful punishment . . . for they cut off those parts whereby I had caused sorrow . . ." (Durant: p. 937).

Abélard, ruined and broken, became a monk. He continued to teach until his views caused further trouble and he retreated to a hermitage where his students built him an oratory called the Paraclete. Héloïse took the veil, but in death they were once again united — buried side by side at the Paraclete, several miles from the vineyards that had helped inspire their love. And if Charles Pierre Péguy (a French writer from the Loire) is not correct in saying "With all their faults, God loves the French the best," perhaps at least Frenchmen are loyal to their own and to their romantic past.

Other eloquent inhabitants gave the Loire a different reputation, establishing its spoken word as the most perfect in all of France. Under the direction of Pierre de Ronsard, considered the father of Lyric poetry in France, several 16th-century poets formed the famous Pléiade group. Ronsard said they were "devoted to revivifying the French language and its use in the noblest literature." His former Greek professor and fellow Pléiade member Jean Dorat — appointed royal poet by Charles IX — couldn't have agreed more. They enlisted the talents of the "Prince of the sonnet," Joachim du Bellay, a native of Anjou who was said to tout the sparkling wines of Saumur. Three hundred years later a French writer named Louis Farigoule would agree with the Pléiade's literary group concept, but he preferred the Loire reds from Chinon, declaring them the proper wines for intellectuals. Monsieur Farigoule (alias Jules Romains) authored novels, plays and verse.

Another prolific product of the Loire, Honoré de Balzac, created the realistic novel. Having studied law and having found it lacking, he secluded himself in a garret and, forced to forgo the famous Vouvray, starved on *vin ordinaire* and bread until he produced his first literary offerings. The effort would one day accord him the accolade "greatest novelist of France." Balzac was born in Tours, the ancient capital of Touraine, both of which were named for the Celtic tribe Turones. The Touraine wine district (home of Vouvray) is often called the Château Country, and for good reason. The feudal lords diminished during the late 15th century and many of their old fort-like castles were transformed by kings (and their descendants) who had fallen in love with France's garden spot during the Hundred Years War. One such fortress at Chinon was where Joan of Arc convinced Charles VII to chase the British out of France (1453). Afterwards, several peculiar men (some even curious) ascended to the French throne, all enthusiastic imbibers of Loire wines. Charles' son Louis XI, "ungainly, homely, melancholy . . . dressed like an impoverished pilgrim . . . scorning the pomp of feudalism, and shocked all thrones with his simplicity . . ." (Will Durant: *The Reformation*, p. 89), was the least thirsty of the bunch and ultimately made France a nation. His taste was inclined toward the austere feudal castle of Langeais, an extraordinary 13th-century military edifice restored by his Minister of State. His inclination toward a nation, however, was an unpopular creation. Its concomitant appendages — internal authority, standardized measurements and currency, governmental alliance with the *bourgeoisie*, a centralized administration that ignored boundaries — annoyed the nobles; and, taxes, the military and suppression of dialects into one language did not please the peasants. Nonetheless, gifted with a bear-trap mind (attending everything but forgetting nothing) and a protean wile — flattering, persuading, ingenuously cajoling through wit, insult or humility — the *sans merci* statesman made them pay to make France great.

Louis XI's son, Charles VIII, inherited some rather less than attractive features too — an unsightly hunchback with thick, puffy lips and Merlin eyes. In spite of such obvious shortcomings, he loved wine, women and war and, laden with Loire wines, marched off to subdue the Kingdom of Naples. The conquest succeeded only in that Charles' retreat included visions of the Italian Renaissance and a few artists, sculptors, landscape gardeners, woodcarvers and architects to duplicate them. Having already restored the castle (1492) at Amboise, Charles VIII ordered the Italians to restyle it as a Renaissance palace. It proved his downfall. Unfortunately poor Charles' agility seems to have been as unfinished as his looks; and, in his haste to attend a tennis match, he lunged through a doorway with an unfastened door. It hit his head and Charles died from a brain injury. He was only twenty-eight.

The crown passed to a nephew, Louis XII. His affability, forthright nature and unusual morality astonished the French people, but in addition he shocked them by lowering taxes, eschewing wealth, and abolishing favoritism. France enjoyed an unprecedented prosperity. When the "Father of the People" died, he bequeathed to his son-in-law, Francis I, among other things, his court painter — Leonardo da Vinci.

It was the loveliest of times and the wines participated in some very good years (1515). "French energy drew from the soil the best wine in Europe; . . ." (Durant: *Reformation;* p. 493.)

Francis I was accustomed to the best. Having been reared at Amboise by an adoring mother devoted to creating a king (she had been widowed at seventeen), he grew fond of the traditional sumptuousness and opulence royalty required. Francis was gallant, courageous and handsome (excepting his nose), the perfect embodiment of the chivalric romances his mother had read to him. Ostensibly, his virility supported his reputation. Brantôme was the quotidian chronicler of important events and people of that day and he recorded: "King Francis loved greatly and too much; for being young and free, he embraced now one, now another, with indifference . . . from which he took the *grande vérole* that shortened his days." His mother was reported to have stated her disgust a bit more graphically: "He was punished where he had sinned." Francis had married in 1515 when he was twenty years old. His wife had borne him seven children when she died in 1524, leaving him the ladies of an entire kingdom to love and discard at his will.

But sensitivity and tenderness were also part of the King's reputation — as well as vanity. He surpassed his contemporary, Henry VIII, in resplendent garments, fur-covered caps and golden bobbles. Perhaps his greatest addiction, however, concerned art. His attraction to artistic beauty financed the French Renaissance, for which he imported the pride of Italy. Da Vinci was even buried at Amboise. Alas, Francis I had a great capacity for all pleasures, but little to govern.

One of his sons, Henry II, was the next king of France (1547–59). At the age of fourteen he married the hapless fourteen-year-old Catherine de Médicis whose Florentine parents had died of the *grande vérole* the month she was born. Catherine inhanced banquets at the French Court by introducing two Florentine accoutrements she brought with her, ice cream making and the fork. Neither endeared her to Henry, who nonetheless sired her ten children. The object of his affection was Diane de Poitiers, a widow twenty years his senior. Their initials were intertwined on every conceivable artifact at the châteaux of Chenonceaux, Amboise and the Louvre, where the *vins de la Loire* were so often featured.

The Loire region closest to Paris — containing Pouilly-sur-Loire, Sancerre, Quincy and Reuilly — is famous for dry white wine. They were said to be the preference of Marie Antoinette, especially Pouilly. The village produces Pouilly-Fumé from the Blanc-fumé grape and should not be confused with the renowned Pouilly wines from Burgundy's Maconnais: Pouilly-Fuissé, Pouilly-Loché, Pouilly-Vinzelles. During the 16th-century Reformation, Sancerre was a Protestant stronghold, as was Saumur, a Loire center for sparkling and all types of wine.

One improvement in the viticultural practices of the Loire has a strange hero. It seems this unlikely was the necessary companion of a wandering Saint Martin as he traversed paths far and wide to the Church owned vineyards. The good brother noted the tender care of growers from place to place and shared the information among viticulturists throughout his travels. It was during such a trip that he tethered his faithful companion, a scraggly donkey, to grape vines at the edge of a property and went on about his business. Saint Martin was absorbed by every facet of vine-growing and wine-making from planting to tasting. He could talk on the subject for hours. This time, however, he stayed in the fields too long. When he returned to his posted friend, the voracious donkey had munched all the shouts and leaves his teeth could reach. Poor Saint Martin stammered and apologized, deeply remorseful about the vines. All the men stood around the nearly naked plant helplessly, and at last, departed. The next spring, almost miraculously, it was those most nibbled parts that sprouted such great rebirth. And *voila!* pruning was thus proclaimed.

LOIRE

Three major wine districts among the nine comprising the Loire region are Touraine, Anjou and Muscadet. Within each there are sub-districts as well, but the references in the book are concerned with the three largest ones which include red, white, rosé and sparkling wines.

District: Touraine two-rain	pleasant, fresh, little wines (reds, whites, and rosés) with general regional appellation	available in the region drink young
Sub-district: Vouvray (white) voo-vrae	varieties available from dry to sparkling or a rich, sweet wine	
Sub-district: Montlouis (white) maw-loo-wee	similar to Vouvray	fish and white meats
Sub-district: Chinon (red) she-nahn	fresh, light, and drunk young	ham, veal Edam, Gouda
Sub-district: Bourgueil (red) boor-gooee	delicate, fruity, bright ruby, best young	poultry, light cheeses
District: Muscadet (white) mues-kahday	pale, dry with little acid, agreeable regional wine	seafoods
District: Anjou ahn-shu		
Sub-district: Saumur (red, white, sparkling) sew, muhr	light, fresh, dry wines	light dishes
Pouilly-Fumé (white) poo-yee few-may	pale straw, dry, fruity, character	sweetbreads, aspics

HISTORIC NAMES LIST

Charlemagne	Burgundy	Corton-Charlemagne
Napoleon	Burgundy	Le Chambertin
	Champagne	Moët & Chandon
Julius Caesar	Bordeaux	Château Ausone
Saint Bernard	Burgundy	Chablis
Huguenots	Burgundy	Pommard
Cistercian monks	Burgundy	Clos de Vougeot
Madame de Pompadour	Champagne	Moët & Chandon
Montaigne	Bordeaux	Château de Montaigne
Montesquieu	Bordeaux	Château de la Brède
Cyrano de Bergerac	Bordeaux	Château Pétrus
Richelieu	Bordeaux	Château Lafite-Rothschild
Samuel Pepys	Bordeaux	Château Haut-Brion
King Henry III	Bordeaux	Château Carbonnieux
Samuel Johnson	Bordeaux	Claret
Commander John Talbot	Bordeaux	Château Talbot
Talleyrand	Bordeaux	Haut-Brion
d'Artagnan	Bordeaux	Claret
Saint Vincent	Bordeaux	Château La Mission-Haut-Brion
Grand Duke Constatine	Bordeaux	Château d'Yquem
Fagon, Louis XIV physician	Burgundy	Nuits Saint Georges
Winston Churchill	Champagne	Pol Roger
Lord Chesterfield	Champagne	Moët & Chandon
Voltaire	Champagne	Ruinart
	Burgundy	Corton

Prince de Conti	Burgundy	Romanée-Conti
Paris cafes	Burgundy	Beaujolais
Robert Walpole	Bordeaux	Château Margaux
Charles de Gaulle	Bordeaux	Château Latour
Marquis de Ségur	Bordeaux	Château Mouton-Rothschild
Thackeray	Bordeaux	Château Gruaud-Larose
King Francis I	Rhône	Tavel
Saint Christopher	Rhône	Hermitage
Fernand Point	Rhône	Côte Rôtie
		Condrieu
		Château Grillet
Pope Clément V	Rhône	Châteauneuf-du-Pape
Abélard	Loire	Muscadet
Joachim du Bellay, poet	Loire	Saumur
Jules Romains, writer	Loire	Chinon
Honoré de Balzac	Loire	Vouvray
Joan of Arc	Loire	Chinon
King Charles VII	Loire	Bourgueil
King Louis XII	Loire	Montlouis
King Francis I	Loire	all Touraine wines
Marie Antoinette	Loire	Pouilly-Fumé

If any of these wines is not available, please ask the restaurateur or your wine merchant for a comparable American wine.

86

INDEX

A

Abbey, Bèze, 9
    Fontenay, 17
    Saulieu, 7
Abélard, 75–77
Akins, Zoe, 65
Albigenses, 66
Almagaire, 9
Amboise, 80, 81, 82
Amour, Saint (Beaujolais), 21
Amoureuses, Les, 11
amphorae, 65
Ampuis, 68
ancien regime, 57
Anjou, 75, 78
Appellation Contrôlée, 2, 31, 62, 69 (def.), 72
Aquitaine, 31, 40
Ausonius, 33, 34
Avignon, 69, 70, 71

B

Babylonian Captivity, 70
Balzac, Honoré de, 78
Bâtard-Montrachet, 16
Beaujolais, 18–21
Beaune, 10, 13
    Côte de, 1, 7, 12, 13, 15, 17
    Hospices de, 13
Bellay, Joachim du, 78
Benedict XII, Pope, 71
Benedictines, 7
Bernard, Saint, 17

Bernardines de l'Abbaye de Notre Dame
    de Tart, 11
Besserat de Bellefon, 56
Blanc-fumé, 82
Blanchots (Chablis), 18
Boiseaumarie, Baron Le Roy de, 70
Bollinger, 59
Boniface VIII, Pope, 70
Bonnes Mares (Morey Saint Denis), 11
    Les (Chambolle), 11
Bordeaux, 31, 32, 33, 34, 35
Bordelais, 32, 33, 40
Boucher, 55
Bougros (Chablis), 18
Bourgogne, 17
Brantôme, 81
Bretons or British, 34, 40, 59
Bristol, Earl of, 42
Brittany, 75, 76
Brouilly (Beaujolais), 21
Bunyan, John, 35
Burgundians, 31
Burgundii, 1, 3
Burgundy, 1, 3, 5

C

Caesar, 3, 21, 33, 53
Cailleret, Le, 16
Capetian dynasty, 40
Carthaginians, 66
Carolingian, 6
Cellini, 72

Celts, 1, 3, 5, 14, 31, 65
Chablis, 1, 17, 18, 45, 75
Chaintre (Mâconnais), 22
chais, 38
Chalonnais, Côte, 1, 17
Chalumeaux, Les, 16
Chambertin, 9, 10
    Gevrey-, 1, 9
Chambolle, 10
Champagne, 53
Champenois, 61
Chardonnay, 18, 20
Charlemagne, 6, 7, 19, 33, 57
    Corton-, 7
Charles VII, King, 79
Charles VIII, King, 80
Charles IX, King, 78
Chassagne, 16
château (def.), 44
Château Ausone, 33
    Belair, 33
    Beychevelle, 37
    Bouscant, 36
    Brassier, 37
    Carbonnieux, 36, 37
    Canon, 33
    Cheval Blanc, 33
    La Conseillante, 44
    l' Evangile, 44
    des Fines-Roche, 72
    Figeac, 33
    Fortia, 72

Grillet, 69
Haut-Brion, 35, 36, 39, 41, 42
Lafite-Rothschild, 38, 39, 40, 41, 42, 43
La Mission-Haut-Brion, 37, 38
Lascombes, 41
Latour, 41, 42, 43
Margaux, 42, 43
Mouton-Rothschild, 43, 44
Châteauneuf-du-Pape, 69, 70, 71, 72
Château Olivier, 36
Pape Clément, 70
Pétrus, 44
Talbot, 40
Château-Vieux-Château-Certan, 44
Château d'Yquem, 45
chef de cave, 56
Chénas (Beaujolais), 21
Chenonceaux, 82
Chesterfield, Lord, 56
chevalier, 13
Chevalier du Tastevin, 8
Chevalier-Montrachet, 15, 16
Chinon, 78, 79
Chiroubles (Beaujolais), 21
Churchill, Winston, 59
Cistercians, 7, 15
claret, 35, 44, 45
clairet, 35
Clément V, Pope, 70, 71
Clément VI, Pope, 71
Clicquot, 56
climats, 2, 4, 5, 14, 32
clos, 9
Clos, Les (Chablis), 18
Clos de Bèze, 9

Clos de Tart, 11
Clos de Vougeot, 8, 9, 33
Clothilde, 6
Clovis, 6
Cluny, 7
communes, 1
conceptualism, 76
Condrieu, 68, 69
Constantine, Grand Duke, 45
Conti, Prince de, 4
Côte Rôtie, 68, 72
Côte d'Or, 1, 16, 32
Cowdray, Viscount, 41
Count of Anjou, 35
Crash, The (Great Depression), 62
crus (growths), 39
crusaders, 66
Cyrano de Bergerac, 31, 44
Czar Alexander, 36

D

Danton, Georges Jacques, 57
d'Artagnan, 31
da Vinci, 72, 80, 82
départements, 1
d'Eperon, Duke, 37
de Medicis, Catherine, 82
de Poitiers, Diane, 82
de Pompadour, Madame, 4, 55
Desmoulins, Camille, 57
Deutz & Geldermann, 59
Dionysus, 22
Dom Pérignon, 53, 55
Dorat, Jean, 78
Druids, 33

Dryden, John, 35
Duke of Normandy, 35
E
Edict of Nantes, 12
Edward III, King, 40
Eginhard, 6
Eleanor of Aquitaine, 34, 40
Elizabeth II, Queen of England, 59
Epernay, 62
F
Farigoule, Louis (alias Jules Romains), 78
Fleurie (Beaujolais), 21
Folatières, Les, 16
Fourneaux (now Taittinger), 56
Francis I, King, 80–82
Franks, 6
frères pontifs, 72
G
Gamay, 21
Gallic-Roman, 3, 5
Gascony, 31, 40
Gaulle, Charles de, 42
George II, King, 56
Givry (Chalonnais), 22
Gironde River, 41
goût de terroire, 69
grande vérole, 81, 82
gravel, 35
Graves, 31, 32, 35, 36, 39
Grenache, 65
Grenouilles (Chablis), 18
Greeks, 65, 66
Guyenne, 31, 39
H
Haut-Médoc, 32
Heidsieck, 56

Héloïse, 76–77
Henry II, King, 82
Henry III, King, 36
Henry VIII, King, 81
Hermitage (Ermitage), 67
Hervey, John (Earl of Bristol), 42
historic personages list, 85–86
Hundred Years' War, 40, 79
Hugo, Victor, 60

J
Jackson, Andrew, 61
Jacobin Club, 57
Joan of Arc, 79
John XXII, Pope, 71
Johnson, Samuel, 35
Julienas (Beaujolais), 21

K
Krug, 54, 59, 60
    Hollier-Larousse, Jeanne, 60

L
La Blonde, 68
La Brune, 68
lahite, 39
Langeais, 79
Lanson, 56
La Pyramide, 68, 69
Legion of Honor, 58
Leipzig, Battle of, 58
Livy, 4
Loché, 22
Loire River, 75
Louis VII, King, 34
Louis XI, King 80
Louis, XII, King, 80

Louis XIV, King (Sun King), 6, 12, 54
Louis XVIII, King, 36
Louis the Pious, 57
Louvre, 82

M
Mâconnais, 1, 21, 22
Marie-Antoinette, 82
Martin, Saint, 83
Massalia (Marseille), 65
Maugiron, 68
Médoc, 31, 32, 38, 39, 41, 45
Mercurey (Chalonnais), 22
Merovingians, 6
méthode champenoise, 62
Meursault, 14, 15
Mirabeau, Comte de, 57
Moët & Chandon, 54, 56, 58
Moët, Jean Remy, 58
mons racemus, 15
mons rachicensis, 15
Montagny (Chalonnais), 22
Montaigne, 31
Montesquieu, 31
Montrachet, 14, 15, 16
Morey-Saint-Denis, 11
Morgan (Beaujolais), 21
Moulin-á-Vent (Beaujolais), 21
mousseux, 75
Mugnier, 10, 11
Mumm, 54, 59
muris saltus, 14, 15
Muscadet, 75, 76
Misigny, Les, 11

N
Nantes, 75
Napoleon, 9, 57, 58
négociant, 2
noblesse de robe, 42, 43
nominalism, 76
Nuit-Saint-Georges, 6

O
oenophile, 3

P
Palace of the Popes, 71
Palais Royal, 54
Paraclete, 77
Paris, 19, 38, 53, 54, 76, 82
Parlement, 43
Parlementaires, 43
Patton, George, 62
Paulée, La, 14
Péguy, Charles Pierre, 78
Pepin, 6
Pepys, 35
Perrier-Jouet, 54
pétillant, 75
petit soupers, 54
Philippe, Duc d'Orleans, 54
Philip IV, King, 70
phylloxera, 5
pieds-à-terre, 37
pierre-à-fusil, 18
Pinot Noir, 5, 21
Plantagenet, 41
    Henry, 35
Pléiade, 78
Pliny, 4

Point, Fernand, 68
Pol Roger, 54, 59
Pomerol, 31, 32, 39, 44
Pommard, 12, 13
Pommery & Greno, 59
Popes, 70
Portugaise, 76
Pouilly-Fuisse, 21
Pouilly-fumé, 82
Pouilly-sur-Loire, 82
pourriture noble, 45
Preuses, Les, (Chablis), 18
Prince Charles, 59
Princess Diana, 59
Prohibition, 62
Punic War, Second, 65
Pucelles, Les, 16
Puligny-Montrachet, 16

Q

Quincy (Loire), 82

R

Rabelais, 72
Rameau, 55
realism, 76
Regency, 54
Reims, 60, 61
Reuilly (Loire), 82

Rhône River, 65
Roederer, 56
Romains, Jules (alias Louis Farigoule), 78
Romans, 1, 3, 4, 6, 14, 21, 22, 66
Romanée-Conti, 4
Romanée, La, 4
Romanée Sanit Vivant, 5
Ronsard, Pierre de, 78
Ruinart, Edmond, 56, 60, 61
Rully (Chalonnais), 22

S

Saint Amour (Beaujolais), 21
Sainte-Christophe, 67
Sancerre (Loire), 82
Saumer (Loire), 82
Sauternes, 44, 45
Ségur, Marquis de, 43
Sévres, 55
Shrewsbury, Earl of (John Talbot), 40
Solutré, 21
Sterimberg, Gaspard de, 66
Syrah, 65

T

Talbot, John, 40
Talleyrand-Périgord, Charles Maurice de, 36
Tain, 67

tastevin, 8
Taittinger, 56
Tavel, 72
Trois Glorieuses, 13
troubadours, 66
Touraine, 78, 79
Tours, 78
Turones, 78, 79

V

Valmur (Chablis), 18
Vaudésir (Chablis), 18
Vercingetorix, 3
Vergisson (Mâconnais), 22
Versailles, 55
Vienna, Congress of, 36
vignoble, 65
Vincent, Saint, 37
vin du pays, 69
vin bourru, 19
Viognier, 65
Voltaire, 55
Vosne-Romanée, 5, 14
Vouvray, 78

W

Walpole, Robert, 42
wine lists: Burgundy 23–29; Bordeaux 47–50; Champagne 63; Rhône 73; Loire 84

90